FUNDAMENTALS OF EFFECTIVE SPEECH COMMUNICATION

Randall Capps
J. Regis O'Connor
Western Kentucky University

UNIVERSITY
PRESS OF
AMERICA

LANHAM • NEW YORK • LONDON

Contents

10 Communicating in Groups 191

Preface

It is possible that a course in speech communication may prove to be one of the most valuable courses you take in college. Why? Because the process of oral communication is certain to occupy a major portion of your life and much of your success will be closely related to the effectiveness with which you communicate with your fellow human beings.

Many writers and researchers have shown the importance of the study of speech communication. Paul Rankin attempted to prove the importance of the spoken word in a study conducted in 1926.[1] He found that average individuals spend 29.5 percent of their waking hours listening, 21.5 percent speaking, 10 percent writing. A more recent study undertook to show how administrators spent their communication time on the job. The results revealed that 16 percent of their time was spent reading, 9 percent writing, 45 percent listening and 30 percent speaking. In other words, skills in oral communication were used more than three times as often as reading and writing skills.[2]

Communication skills are important for technical workers as well as for administrators. The Menninger Clinic studies found that 70 percent of the workers who lose their jobs lose them not because they lack the technical knowledge to perform their assignment but because they fail to communicate clearly.[3] Thus, job security may be closely related to communication behavior.

Some people assume that human beings are born with speech communication ability. They believe that nothing can be done to improve their communication skills. Fortunately, speech communication skills are learned and may be improved if individuals are willing to discipline themselves. The underlying assumption in this class, then, is that oral communication skills are learned and that these skills can be improved through

[1]Paul Tory Rankin, "The Measurement of the Ability to Understand Spoken Language" (unpublished Ph.D. dissertation, University of Michigan, 1926).
[2]Jeffrey Auer, "Speech is A Social Force," *National Education Association Journal* XLIX (November, 1960): 22–24.
[3]Ibid.

directed learning and supervised practice. This text is intended to serve as a guide for you to follow in improving your ability to communicate more effectively.

Many basic speech courses, taught by a number of faculty are a collection of traditional and modern thought, of public speaking and discussion, of theory and practice. This text is an attempt to fuse these elements into a unified form that will promote faculty satisfaction and student understanding. The chapters have been written by a number of experienced speech instructors, each of whom has had experience teaching oral communication. Each author has approached his chapter(s) with a working knowledge of the common goals of the course as well as with a special dedication to the subject matter of his chapter. We consider the kind of cohesiveness that grows from diversity of viewpoints as a distinct strength of this text. The editors attempted to amalgamate certain differences in emphasis that occasionally occurred, but those that remain should serve as a challenge, both to the alert student, and to classroom instructors who may be questioned about those differences.

Each teacher inevitably approaches the basic speech course in his or her own way. This book is our way of recognizing that fact.

The author of each chapter is raising several philosophical questions which you should seriously consider. These questions are not printed as such in the chapters, but may be the most important ones that you will consider during this course. They are questions like: Is it ever right to deceive a listener in any way? Must I always mention the arguments opposed to my position? Are there times when I must make my opinion known? Are there times when I should remain silent? Such questions relate to the ethics (morality) of the communication process; they are important because the ability to communicate effectively is a powerful tool which must not be misused. Those who teach this skill must always be concerned, therefore, that they not only teach effective communication, but *right* communication. The ancient Roman Cato defined the orator as "the good man, skilled in speaking." In the wake of Watergate, a respect for truth in communication must surely be seen as the greatest need of those who speak in public.

We are grateful to several authors and publishers who allowed us to use their copyrighted material.

The editors wish to acknowledge several people who have been especially helpful in the preparation of this text; Pat O'Connor who did the illustrations and Fonzole Childress who patiently typed the original drafts. Mrs. Betty De Armond and Mrs. Elizabeth Whitfield completed the final typing and composition, and James Flynn was kind enough to proofread the finished copy. Other colleagues and students have offered advice and encouragement which was always appreciated.

Randall Capps
J. Regis O'Connor

Understanding the Nature of Communication*

1

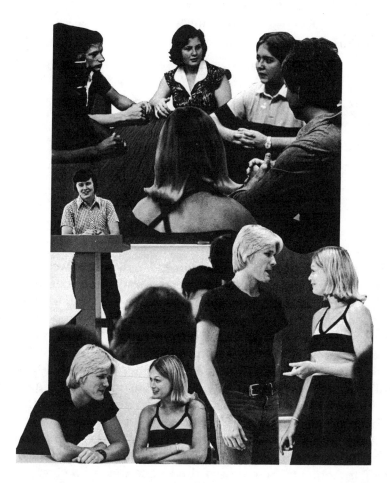

*By Carley H. Dodd.

OBJECTIVES ❧

After completing this chapter, you should be able to:

1. *Define* communication.
2. *Locate* and *diagram* key elements of the communication process.
3. *Explain* motivations for speaking.
4. *Describe* elements of intrapersonal, interpersonal, public, and cross-cultural communication.
5. *Discuss* problems in perception.
6. *Note* the importance of networks in small group communication.
7. *List* general steps in developing a speaking campaign.

A high school principal announces a new sick leave policy. If the teachers have questions, he requests their consultation. Later, three teachers meet jointly with the principal in his office and object to the new policy. After the conversation the three teachers agree the principal hardly heard a word they said. Meanwhile, the principal congratulates himself for his "openness." Did communication fail? A teacher lectures enthusiastically on a favorite topic in a course, but students complain of the terminology and jargon they could not understand. What aspect of communication faltered? A religious speaker addresses a high school audience and speaks on current issues in scholarly areas of theology. Some of the listeners are overheard later to bemoan their wasted time since the speaker was "over their heads." Why was their time wasted? Such situations occur repeatedly. Answers to questions about communication failures are complex and require an understanding of the process of communication.

Even our most sincere efforts at communication lead to misunderstanding. Consider the following humorous essay on communication and then ask yourself if your communication needs improvement:

They Shoot Language, Don't They?

The way some people blubber and snort off words, one sometimes wonders if they even know what they mean. One lady I knew talked so fast that I never could insert even a simple "Uh-huh," much less an unexpected cough (although there were lots of yawns). It seems that some people never realize they are boring and that their unappealing conversation stems from not thinking before speaking.

Some phrases sound right until you consider what they mean. For example, the late nationally known basketball coach, E. A. Diddle, was reported to have remarked to his players, "All right boys, line up alphabetically by height." When you travel, you may come across a sign somewhere in a roadside park that reads "People Without Dogs On a Leash Not Permitted." Perhaps the park commissioner never realized that the admonition prevents persons without dogs from ever entering the premises.

Communication about people and about current ideas can be entertaining. A bumper sticker smeared on the back of a car remarked about Euell Gibbons of the Grape Nuts commercial and author of six books on surviving in nature: "SAVE OUR FORESTS—EXTRACT EUELL GIBBONS' TEETH."

Children used to chant the verse "Sticks and stones may hurt my bones but words can never touch me." For children, that phrase may be true, because they do not always know what adult language means. But as meanings become codified and categorized for the mature, let us remember that words can rip apart like a vulture tearing at its carrion, or words can heal and bind together like a finely sewn surgical stitch. So try harder for better communication.

In a simple way, this essay points to an almost universal need to monitor our communication constantly.

This chapter introduces basic concepts in speech communication. Such an introduction will show the overall picture of the communication process and will help explain communication failures like those cited above. Admittedly, what we call a process can be described only as a snapshot, but the picture provides a vantage point from which to view and to understand the inter-working of communication factors.

This chapter first defines the communication process, thereby briefly introducing a core of terminology and concepts for understanding the process. The second section furnishes a contextual view of the communication process. In this section you will discover the basic communication contexts and unique characteristics of the one-to-one, small group, public communication, and cross-cultural communication situations. Research findings, included in this discussion, will offer additional insight into basic communication concepts. The third section covers personal awareness of communication habits and extends the understanding of vital concepts to the practical aspects of everyday communication.

A Definitional View of Communication

The roots of the word *communication* (*communis*, or common) accurately portray its purpose. In communication the speaker is attempting to "be one" with the listener. In the process of "being one" we develop a communion, a transaction, a dialogue. At its foundation, communication involves a uniting and exchanging of thoughts. As a result, the speaker is obligated to create a clear picture of reality to stimulate listeners and to "make common" his or her thoughts.[1] The goal of

---

[1]For a fuller discussion of the importance of painting pictures of reality in communication, see Carl Kell and Larry Winn, *Guidebook in Public Communication* (Dubuque, Iowa: Kendall/Hunt Publishing Co., 1976), pp. 9–11.

communication is to secure an overlap of information experience, as illustrated in Figure 1.1.

How this process of communication occurs is the subject of this chapter. Basically, we communicate by using the tools available to us, namely symbols. Verbal and nonverbal language are essentially sets of commonly accepted symbols to which we attach meaning. Communication involves a person transmitting those language symbols through some method to another person. The process resembles a telegraph operator transmitting a message to a telegraph operator in another city who deciphers the message. Communication is not only transactional (involving a two-way process) and symbolic (requiring use of a symbolic code) but communication usually brings about some effects. Our lives do not remain unaffected by the symbolic world around us. When receiving a telegraphed birthday wish, we usually experience feelings of appreciation often to the point of verbally expressing excitement.

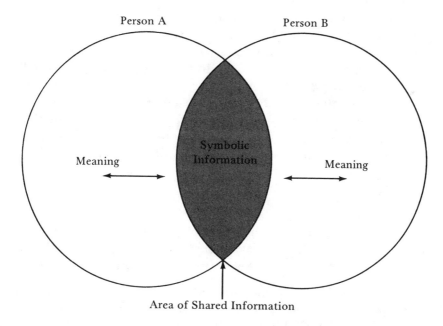

Figure 1.1

Thus, we define speech communication as *the transmission and reception of symbolic stimuli, such as words and gestures, acting symbolically to elicit meaning. The effect may be instrumental or direct and results in feedback.* Each part of this definition contains key elements of the communication process. As you consider the following description of the key elements, you should develop further insight into problems and processes of communication.

Transmission and Reception

Thoughts and ideas do not magically flow from point *A* to point *B*. Rather, a person employs the available language and acceptable code system. Thought is translated into symbols and is spread by some form of transmission. A person may use visual stimuli (such as written words or gestures) or vocal stimuli (such as spoken words). During the transmitting process, many physiological, neurological, and psychological factors are involved.[2] The entire process of translation from thought to symbol is called *encoding*.

Reception is not just a process of hearing or seeing, but like transmission it involves a complex interaction of physiological, neurological, and psychological factors. When information is received it is processed. Studies indicate that most individuals remember 15 percent of what they hear, 75 percent of what they see and 90 percent of what they see and hear. The composite process of receiving and processing incoming information is called *decoding*. Chapter 7 of this text describes practical aspects of better listening in reception of information.

Symbolic Stimuli

VERBAL STIMULI   When speaking and listening one has a pool of verbal vocabulary available for use. Simply speaking or writing the appropriate words in proper sequence will signal

---

[2]While the average person thinks that communication is primarily a "natural" process, evidence points to the complexity of human transaction as a learned phenomenon capable of alteration. For a fuller discussion see George A. Borden, Richard B. Gregg, and Theodore G. Grove, *Speech Behavior and Human Interaction* (Englewood Cliffs, N.J.: Prentice-Hall, 1969).

intended meanings. If two people share the same set of verbal symbols, in the form of vocabulary, and the same grammatical structure, communication approaches the ideal. To the extent that individuals do not share these aspects, communication becomes less than ideal.[3] For example, suppose a North American told an Ashanti tribesman about space vehicles. Since space travel is not a part of the verbal pool of symbols of the Ashanti, one predicts a severely limited conversation about space vehicles, unless there is extended elaboration. Yet, a college student and his best friend would probably have little difficulty discussing space vehicles, since that domain of technology is common to both.

NONVERBAL STIMULI Just as verbal stimuli act symbolically to elicit meaning, another set of stimuli operates in communication—nonverbal stimuli. Nonverbal behaviors refer to one's use of body, time, and space. Like the verbal code, nonverbal codes also stimulate meanings. The point is well illustrated by deaf persons who communicate by a highly formalized, totally nonverbal code system. In a far more informal manner, everyone uses nonverbal behavior to communicate. Some of these behaviors elicit meaning implicitly (such as a beckoning gesture), others emerge in coordination with verbal communication as auxiliary messages, such as a frown accompanying words of disappointment. Nonverbal communication breaks into several subcategories:

1. *Body language.* The study of body language is called *kinesics.* Kinesic behavior consists of body position, body orientation, facial expressions, gestures, and the like. Most kinesic behaviors alone are highly ambiguous and take their meaning only in the total context of one's conversation or speech.[4]

[3]The term *verbal communication* refers to the use of *oral or written* words. See also Chapter 4 on language.

[4]For a full discussion of the relationship between kinesics and spoken language, see Ray L. Birdwhistell, "Some Relations between American Kinesics and Spoken American English," in Alfred G. Smith, ed., *Communication and Culture* (New York: Holt, Rinehart and Winston, 1966), pp. 182–89; Albert Mehrabian, *Silent Language* (Belmont, Ca.: Wadsworth, 1971).

2. *Use of space.* Humans also communicate through their use of space. The study of spatial communication is called *proxemics.* How far or how close one stands from others can often strongly influence the outcome of a conversation. For example, the normal North American zone for standing conversation is about three feet. To converse at a lesser distance is to invade one's privacy and appear quite obtrusive. To stand at a greater distance than normal is to appear unfriendly and "distant." Public speakers who are physically removed from the audience both by distance and by a speaker's stand may inadvertently create a perceived psychological gap. Culture influences highly our expectations of appropriate proxemic distances.

3. *Eye movements.* Practical experience as well as research indicates the importance of both eye movements and eye contact. *Oculesic* research and observation reveals that North Americans tend to trust those who meet them "eye to eye." Lack of eye contact signals distrust. Furthermore, eye movements indicate a variety of messages, such as disgust, surprise, boredom, and so forth.

4. *Time.* The study of time or temporality is called *chronemics.* Perception of time is highly culture-bound, a fact leading to countless instances of cross-cultural misunderstanding. In North America, violations of temporal observances speak loudly. For example, tardiness to a business appointment can create innumerable negative impressions about the latecomer. Those nonverbal impressions may outweigh the verbal message and damage the relationship. When a speaker arrives late, certain messages are received, depending on the speaker's identity. A speech that is too long or too short for the occasion carries unfavorable nonverbal connotations.

PARALINGUISTIC STIMULI   In addition to verbal and nonverbal stimuli acting symbolically to elicit meaning in communication, a third type of stimulus also evokes meaning. Paralanguage is the set of vocal, nonvocabulary utterances that carry meaning.[5] Such utterances include inflections, rate, pitch, volume, grunts, hmms, uh-huhs, and sighs. Were it not for paralinguistic stimuli, many messages would be imprecise, if not totally incomprehensible. For instance, questions reflect a shift in inflection at the end of the sentence. Phone conversations are laden with "uh-huh," "hmm," and "oo." We even refer to speakers as having a "tone of disgust." These paralinguistic attributes convey meanings in themselves and may outweigh a speaker's actual words. Individuals engaged in argument testify to the paralinguistic features of speech when they indicate, "It's not *what* you said, it's the *way* you said it."

Communication Effects

The effects or outcomes of communication are directly related to why people speak. If you could replay past communication events and simultaneously peer into our communication future, what would you observe? You would see people speaking and listening to satisfy personal needs, to establish relationships, to understand the same things, to believe what is understood, and occasionally to entertain. These purposes of human speech can also be viewed in light of psychological, sociological, and cultural motivations.[6] If you consider the outcomes in relation to the purpose of speech, you should have a more thorough outlook on communication effects.

EFFECTS OF SPEAKING TO SATISFY PERSONAL NEEDS   When we make requests and issue commands, we are using communication to satisfy needs. When someone declares, "Pass me the salt," communication is used to enact a need fulfillment. Even assertions such as "I like chocolate ice cream" may be intended to fill some personal need ("since I like chocolate ice cream, why not give me some"). Communication that focuses the spotlight

[5]Other terms used to describe these phenomena are *metalanguage* and *extraverbal communication*.

[6]Thomas Scheidel, *Speech Communication and Human Interaction* (Glenview, Ill.: Scott, Foresman and Co., 1972).

totally on the speaker (measured by frequent use of self-reference words), however, might soon become ineffectual. Once communication becomes overwhelmingly egocentric and the speaker "talks to hear himself talk," that person's speaking may be ignored.

EFFECTS OF SPEAKING TO ESTABLISH RELATIONSHIPS   A significant portion of your day is spent establishing and maintaining rapport. Even simple greetings like "How are you?" serve to recognize others and to provide a link in your relationship with others. Several years ago, a field study was conducted of telephone calls of business executives. The research revealed that one major purpose of calls from one executive to another within the same organization was to maintain friendly ties. Apparently, a certain amount of rapport-building signals a healthy relationship. Effects of rapport-building communication also include increased trust and liking.

EFFECTS OF SPEAKING TO CREATE UNDERSTANDING   We use speech to share with others significant information about people, things, places, events, and personal feelings. Such speech informs listeners. The effects of information-sharing are two-fold: (1) The information may serve an awareness function satisfying our need to know about our environment;[7] and (2) Awareness at one point in time may set the stage upon which later persuasive messages build.[8] When information is used as a stepping stone for later persuasion, it is called *instrumental communication*.

EFFECTS OF SPEAKING TO CREATE CHANGE   We also use persuasive messages to enact change. Messages offering solutions to problems or satisfaction for personal needs are perceived as motivational. For example, toothpaste advertising

[7]Daniel Katz, "The Functional Approach to the Study of Attitudes," *Public Opinion Quarterly* 24 (1960): 163–204.

[8]In the spread of new products and services it is a well-documented fact that potential buyers go through the decision-making stages of awareness, evaluation, and finally persuasion where the individual decides to adopt or reject. See Everett M. Rogers and F. Floyd Shoemaker, *Communication of Innovations* (New York: Free Press, 1971).

promising whiter teeth appeals to one's need to be liked and thus motivates change. However, effects of persuasive messages are mixed. In some cases, communication may be instrumental, thus seeking to gain acceptance for one idea which will be a building block for a later point of persuasion. In other cases, persuasive messages may be direct, implying an immediate change. For instance, religious speakers may seek direct effects in terms of conversion. However, a central point of persuasion theory underscores that persuasive effectiveness depends on receivers' prior attitudes, education, age, sex, and personality characteristics.

EFFECTS OF SPEAKING TO ENTERTAIN   Entertaining speeches include joke-telling, storytelling, and "visiting" communication (such as small talk, dormitory rapping, and coffee break conversation). Entertaining communication serves not only its entertaining purpose but produces less obvious effects. Bob Hope's political jokes entertain but also provide a certain amount of reinforcement for those who support or deny the point of the joke. A third-grade teacher reading aloud fairy tales to a class not only entertains but reinforces various beliefs, such as "good wins over evil."

Feedback

Communication, as a two-way process, involves feedback. Feedback is the sum total of the receiver's reactions to the message and its sender. Feedback takes many forms—sighs, yawns, applause, widening of eyes, shrug of the shoulders, yelling, or even leaving the sender's presence. Whatever form it takes, feedback serves as an "instrument panel" allowing senders to monitor their communication and to make appropriate adjustments.

A Structural View of Communication Elements

In addition to a definition of communication, a communication model structurally describes communication in terms of its essential components. Just as a stereo player has essential parts constituting the total player set, communication has essential elements intertwined to produce the total process we have defined as communication. The model in Figure 1.2 demonstrates essential communication elements. As you examine the model, notice the structural relationships of the parts in relation to our earlier definition.

Communication consists of six basic elements: sender, message, channel, receiver, effects, and feedback.[9] The source (sender) originates the message and employs various communication skills in implementing it. The message consists of sym-

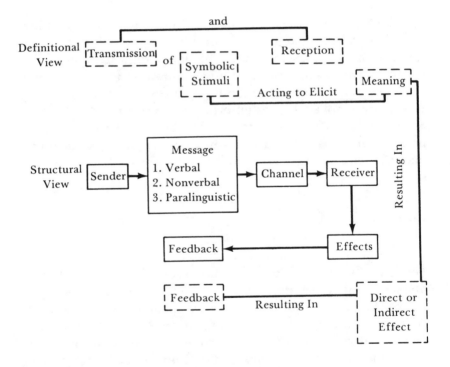

Figure 1.2   *A Definitional View Coordinated With a Structured View of Communication*

[9]David K. Berlo, *The Process of Communication* (New York: Holt, Rinehart and Winston, 1960). Berlo's original model incorporates only the source, message, channel, and receiver. Although he clearly outlined the role of feedback, Berlo did not include feedback or effect in his model.

bolic stimuli (verbal, nonverbal, paralinguistic) transmitted over a channel, either face-to-face or through mass media. The receiver decodes the stimuii. The effects of the message upon the receiver begin the process of feedback. During the feedback process the receiver in fact becomes the sender and the sender becomes the receiver.

A Contextual View of Communication

Human communication does not occur in a vacuum. Rather, communication is ordered by situation and context. The term *context* refers to levels or types of communication according to setting, channel, and number of people involved. The most fundamental level incorporates communication within each individual, called intrapersonal communication. When two or more people interact, interpersonal communication occurs. Public communication involves the speaker-audience context in which audience attention is polarized toward a central figure, the speaker. Finally, cross-cultural communication highlights communication occurring in still another context—the cultural setting.

Intrapersonal Communication

Intrapersonal communication focuses upon the individual as the unit of analysis. At this level we refer to those features within the individual that relate to the processing, transmission, and reception of information. Although these features involve complex neurological and physiological aspects, understanding psychological aspects provides an especially helpful beginning point in developing basic concepts in communication.

One particularly important psychological feature of the intrapersonal system lies in the nature of *perception*. We all have a "psychological screen" through which information is sifted. Information that an individual receives is consequently filtered and perceived in light of past experiences, attitudes, and expectations. For example, if I am a poor golfer and have developed a dislike for golf, the next time I hear the word *golf* I may have a strong emotional reaction. Contrast that reaction with the feelings that professional golfer Johnny Miller experiences upon hearing the same word. Why do we each respond differently to the same word? The difference is explained in our perception. However, our perceptions also can distort reality. Let us examine two particular perceptual problems that frequently occur.

DISTORTION BY CONTEXT   We evaluate information in light of the total context. For example, a speech moderately favoring consumerism presented before an avid consumer audience whose meeting room is lined with banners, slogans, and consumer displays (context) can lead individuals who hear the speech to perceive the speech as more extreme toward consumerism than is actually the case. Individuals evaluate messages in relation to the surroundings in which that message is uttered. Figure 1.3 illustrates this principle. The diagonal line

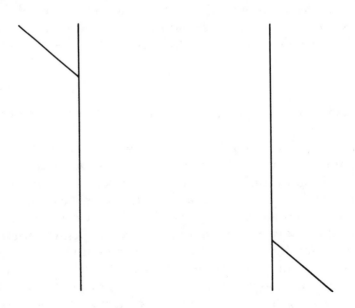

Figure 1.3   *Although the diagonal line is straight, it appears offset.*

appears offset though the line is perfectly straight; our perception of the line is thus distorted.

DISTORTION BY PREMATURE CLOSURE   The principle of closure refers to forming general impressions from limited information or from prior expectations. We assume something to be what it is not. Figure 1.4 appears to be a triangle. Actually, the figure consists only of three unconnected dots. "Hasty generalization" results from misunderstanding the fact that events and ideas are not always as they appear.

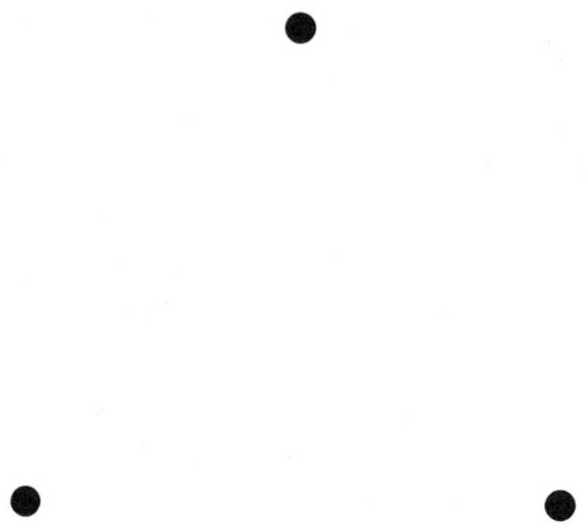

Figure 1.4   *By the principle of closure we assume this to be a triangle. Actually, we only have three unconnected dots.*

Interpersonal Communication

Interpersonal communication focuses upon two or more individuals interacting verbally and nonverbally in a face-to-face situation. Traditionally, this level of communication involves two basic classifications: dyadic communication and small group communication. Each of these two levels contains unique characteristics warranting special attention.

DYADIC COMMUNICATION   Dyadic communication refers to two persons engaged in dialogue, or one-to-one communication. Even in this basic encounter, dynamic communication features operate. One important concept is balance theory. For instance, suppose you are talking with a good friend, who, you have just discovered, is deeply involved in a political party you despise. You like your friend, but, remember, she likes a political party you dislike. Given this unbalanced state of relationships, balance theory predicts you will communicate to change attitudes toward the topic or toward the other person. In other words, you may reject your future friendship or you may change your feelings positively toward the political party.[10]

Another important consideration in dyadic communication centers on status and roles. Status refers to social position, rank, or standing. Role behavior refers to a behavior one performs or is expected to perform regularly. For instance, if you were interviewing for a new job, the role of the personnel manager would be obvious even to the point of predicting his or her communication behavior: "We'll give this every consideration," "As soon as we firm up our plans, we'll let you know," and so on. Of course, status also operates in dyadic situations as in the case of your conversing with your employer. Depending upon the work atmosphere and the level of management your employer holds, the dyad might be characterized as one of dominance and submission. Or, in the circumstance of a doctor-patient dyad, the variables of role and status operate simultaneously: respective roles and status ranks are maintained.[11]

SMALL GROUP COMMUNICATION   A second type of interpersonal communication setting is the small group. Small groups usually consist of three to twenty-five members, although most small groups contain six to twelve members.[12] Generally, researchers classify groups according to their purpose: problem-solving, information-sharing, or therapy. Communication research on small groups reveals that numerous variables interact dynamically yielding various outcomes.

---

[10]See Chapter 9 for a fuller discussion of balance theory.

[11]Chapter 7 describes interpersonal aspects of listening. Chapter 9 also discusses the concepts of role and status.

[12]Dean C. Barnlund and Franklyn S. Haiman, *The Dynamics of Discussion* (Boston: Houghton Mifflin, 1960).

Among these variables are roles, status, leadership types, frequency of interaction, type of interaction, propinquity (physical distance), cohesiveness, group purpose, and networks or channels of communication. A few research findings illustrate the importance of some of the above variables:

1. Frequency of one's communication is related to one's emergence as a leader.
2. High authoritarian leadership sometimes yields efficient production of the group task but leaves group members feeling emotionally "unsatisfied."
3. The greater the cohesiveness of a small group the greater the pressure to conform to the norms and rules of the group.
4. Individuals sitting in close proximity to each other tend to have greater interpersonal liking and preference for each other than do persons sitting more remotely (for example, across the table). (This generalization has enormous implications for labor-management bargaining since sitting across from one's "opponent" is an initial barrier.)

Readers can also find hundreds of research findings and generalizations important to the formation, maintenance, and dissolution of small groups.[13]

Communication networks also influence the maintenance of small groups. Communication networks refer to the lines of communication open to members in the small group. Some of the most frequent arrangements are shown in Figure 1.5. Research indicates that the arrangement of members, dictating "who can talk with whom," affects the emergence of leadership. Shaw indicates, for example, that a person who occupies a central position in one of these networks (such as the wheel and the Y) is more likely to emerge as a group leader.[14] Conversely, the person on the periphery of group interaction tends to be isolated by group members. Try your own experiment by ar-

[13]See Marvin E. Shaw, *Group Dynamics,* 2nd ed. (New York: McGraw-Hill, 1976); Robert S. Cathcart and Larry A. Samovar, *Small Group Communication: A Reader,* 2d ed. (Dubuque, Iowa: William C. Brown, 1974).

[14]Shaw, *Group Dynamics,* pp. 139–40.

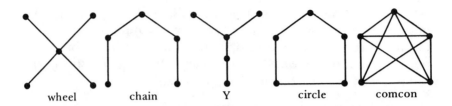

wheel   chain   Y   circle   comcon

Figure 1.5

ranging the chairs in a circle and then placing some person on
the outside or edge of a group. Notice the amount of communication directed toward him or originating from him. Also note
his behavior—he may in fact move his chair closer or withdraw
entirely from communication with the group. Chapter 10 discusses concepts in group problem-solving discussions.

Public Communication

A third context of communication centers on public communication. In this level of communication a central figure, the
speaker, draws attention toward a set of ideas relevant to the
speaker, the audience, or both. Examples range from
clubhouse speeches to presidential addresses. From the observations of ancient philosophers to present research in public
speaking, a large body of knowledge exists regarding effective
oral communication in a public setting. We know, for instance,
that the speaker brings to each speaking event a degree of
believability or credibility (called ethos by Aristotle). This affects the audience by the sheer weight of personality, reputation, and other character-related factors associated with the
speaker prior to and during his or her presentation. Researchers have listed several factors that determine source credibility. Speaker credibility results partly from factors external to
the speech itself, such as the speaker's physical attraction, prior
education, occupation, and moral characteristics (including
religious affiliation, marital status, and even number of arrests).

Speaker credibility also stems from factors within the speech, such as use of evidence and logic, quality of organization, and language usage.[15]

Research concerning the message in a public speech has likewise been significant. First, concrete language appears more effective than abstract language, unless the speaker is deliberately using ambiguity and vagueness (as in the case of a political campaigner who chooses to avoid specificity and clarity). Second, when presenting two sides of an issue in a single speech, research indicates the advantage of first presenting the side with which the audience initially agrees.[16] Third, the decision to present pro and con arguments on a topic or to present only one side of an issue depends upon the audience. If the audience is fairly intelligent and is likely to hear the other side of the issue at some later time, it is better to present both the pro and con sides of the issue. Other nonverbal message effects, such as the use of gestures and paralinguistic aspects of vocal delivery (intonation, pitch, loudness, rate), are also important in public speaking.

One final consideration in public speaking centers on audience analysis. In general, most communication attempts involve some form of audience analysis resulting in an awareness of audience attitude, various demographic characteristics (such as age, residence, education level, socioeconomic status), cultural background, and audience expectations. Speakers should conduct as much audience analysis as possible, since the more they know about their audience the better they can direct their goals to the audience's needs and values. For instance, suppose you were invited to speak at a PTA in your city on the topic of increasing teachers' salaries, and you intend to speak "for" that issue. Your first job would be to determine the composition of your audience and to learn as much as possible about their attitudes. You might discover, for example, that the audience is

[15]Gerald R. Miller, *An Introduction to Speech Communication* (Indianapolis: Bobbs-Merrill, 1972), pp. 39–44. See also Chapter 8 of this text for a fuller discussion of ethos.

[16]Arthur Cohen, *Attitude Change and Social Influence* (New York: Basic Books, 1964), pp. 11–15.

divided into persons for, against, and undecided about raising teachers' salaries:

For	Undecided	Against
25%	45%	30%

Coupling this knowledge with information on demographic characteristics, you might conclude that the best strategy is to aim the speech toward those undecided on the issue while simultaneously strengthening the beliefs of the "for" group. With maximum success this strategy offers a 70 percent to 30 percent margin in this example.

To begin the process of change in an "against" group, one useful strategy is to employ arguments and examples geared toward respected leaders of the group. If the leaders change, you have maximized your chances for total change. Of course, change often occurs over a period of time and not in one performance, though a single speech may be an instrumental factor causing later persuasion. Sometimes if a speaker "pushes too hard," however, a *boomerang* effect occurs and the reaction is opposite to that desired by the speaker.

Cross-cultural Communication

Communication can be investigated not only on an individual, dyadic, group, or public level, but also on a cultural level. The study of cross-cultural communication (also called intercultural communication) examines cultural and social systems variables as they influence communication. This area of study and research includes international communication (referring to communication among nations on a political level), intracultural communication (communication within a culture), interracial communication (between two different races), interethnic communication (between two minority ethnic groups, for example, Chicano-black), and contracultural communication (where a subgroup in a dominant culture arises against the dominant group).

Certain cultural peculiarities within and between cultures affect the communication that occurs. Nonverbal dimensions of communication, especially time and space, are certainly key variables in cross-cultural interaction, as are the various aspects of kinesics (body movement). The particular cultural modes of behavior (dress, food habits, transportation, and so on), culturally accepted personality types, and world view represent additional variables influencing cross-cultural communication.[17]

One other perspective of cross-cultural communication deserves mention, an area called diffusion of innovations. An innovation is anything new that people can use tangibly or think about mentally. Diffusion of innovation means the spread of anything new through speaking and listening. In dealing with other cultures researchers find that ideas or technology spread through different types of people, or in other words, diffuse through different channels of communication. For instance, sometimes the best strategy in communicating a message in a village is to find the person most respected in that village and get him to help spread your message. Messages should also be constructed with an awareness of norms and values of the culture group.

A Self-awareness View of Communication

It is hoped that the concepts already introduced in this chapter have caused you to think about your own communication. After all, most people usually want to be understood and to understand others. This section of the chapter points toward self-awareness of communication habits. Questions in this section lead to applications of concepts presented earlier in this chapter.

[17]Carley H. Dodd, *Perspectives on Cross-Cultural Communication* (Dubuque, Iowa: Kendall/Hunt Publishing Co., 1977).

Do You Assume Your Viewpoints Are Universal?

Too often individuals assume that their feelings toward a topic represent others' feelings. This over-generalization leads to an egocentric view of the world and makes such an individual susceptible to being perceived as narrow-minded, bigoted, boring, and unreasonable. When people disagree with such an individual, the disagreement is viewed as a personal attack and can lead to hostile retaliation.

Do You Communicate Slanted Information?

One frequently receives slanted reports but also unwittingly communicates slanted information. Whether consciously or unknowingly, coloration stems from omitting or adding details, and using emotionally loaded words. Consider the following three accounts of the same story. Mark down expressions that contribute to a slanted narration.

> *A person who gave his name as John K. Bolger and his age as 17 was brought by Patrolman Arthur Smith to the Fifth Precinct Station at 5:32 P.M. yesterday in handcuffs. Patrolman Smith reported that at 5:05 he had seen Bolger run out the door of the Daly Drugstore with a pistol in his hand, and that a second or two later the proprietor, William Daly, 66, appeared, with blood on his forehead, shouting "Stop, thief!" According to Patrolman Smith, Mr. Daly reported that Bolger had struck him on the head with a pistol, taken $15 from the cash register drawer, and run through the front door. In Bolger's jacket pocket the police found $15.*

> *Late yesterday a leather-jacketed, teen-age hoodlum named Bolger pistol whipped an elderly pharmacist in his neighborhood drugstore, scooped up some money, and made a mad dash straight into the arms of a passing police officer. The loot was recovered.*

> *Yesterday shortly before dinnertime a half-starved youth named John K. Bolger was dragged to the Fifth Precinct*

lockup and charged with armed robbery and felonious assault on the unsupported complaint of a store-owner who claimed that Mr. Bolger had attacked him and taken a few dollars from the firm's cash drawer. The cop who hauled Mr. Bolger to the stationhouse had been loitering in front of the business establishment at the time.

Do the slanted portions occur from the words, the context, or from a combination of factors? Is it possible to make a verbal report in which no slanting occurs?[18]

Do You Place Yourself in the Other Person's Shoes?

We frequently assume that listeners automatically understand our words just because we speak. Ask yourself several questions. Do I assume that if what I say is clear to me it is clear to others? Do I try to understand the other person's total situation and feelings? Do I encourage discussion and questions to check the other person's understanding of what I told him?

Summary

This chapter introduced basic concepts of speech communication. Understanding basic touchstones should place the reader at a vantage point from which to view the inter-workings of the communication process. Although the chapter does not exhaust introductory notions in speech communication, the chapters throughout the remainder of this text will deal in more depth with practical usage of many of the concepts mentioned in this chapter.

Specifically, Chapter 2 examines the communication sender. That chapter discusses intrapersonal anxiety about

[18]Chapter 4 of this text discusses numerous other semantic problems of language usage.

speaking and suggests ways of securing listeners' attention. Chapters 3, 4, 5, and 6 deal with specific aspects of public communication: organizing a message, utilizing language in a message, delivering a message, and illustrating a message. Chapter 7 deals with the reception of information. Chapter 8 then explains a special type of public communication, persuasion. Chapter 9 provides a framework both for transmission and reception within one-to-one communication. Chapter 10 discusses small group communication.

Contacting Your Audience in Speaking*

*By Randall Capps and J. Regis O'Connor.

OBJECTIVES ✂

After completing this chapter, you should be able to:

1. *Understand* the nature of speech communication apprehension.
2. *Analyze* your own problems with communication apprehension.
3. *Discuss* the nature of audience attention in a public speaking situation.
4. *Identify* the attention devices commonly used in public speaking.
5. *Develop* specific attention devices for use in your own speeches.

Two problems immediately confront most beginning public speakers: "How can I control my communication apprehension or stage fright?" and "How can I capture and hold the attention of my audience?" This chapter will deal with both of these problems. We will consider stage fright first since it is usually the first concern of many beginning speakers. Many of you probably feel that you aren't really very concerned about gaining your listeners' attention until after you have conquered your stage fright. For most beginning speakers, however, the very process of trying to capture audience attention can help dissipate stage fright. Thus, these two psychological aspects of public speaking are considered together in a single chapter. Once you have developed the mental attitude as a speaker that says: "I have a message that interests and excites me, and I'm going to do everything I can to focus my listeners' attention and interest on my topic. . . ," stage fright disappears to a large extent.

Part I: Communication Apprehension

Beginning speakers often encounter a nervous condition called speech communication apprehension. Few students experience no apprehension and more than 50 percent experience moderate or severe problems. Stage fright symptoms include dryness of throat or mouth, forgetting, tension of the abdominal region, inability to produce voice, stuttering or stammering, tremors of knees and hands, weak voice, excessive perspiration, accelerated heart rate, speech rate too fast or too slow, stomach upset, difficulty in breathing, inability to look at the audience, feeling that the audience is disapproving, inability to finish speaking, excessive hesitation, and dread before speaking.[1] One researcher found that severe apprehension caused a limited verbal output, a constricted vocabulary, and a decided increase in the number of speaking errors.[2]

Although communication apprehension is a particular problem with beginning speakers, it often plagues even experienced speakers but in lesser degrees. Some speech authorities feel that a certain amount of apprehension is good because it shows the speaker is interested in doing a good job in putting his or her ideas across in the most effective manner possible.

One of the main causes of communication apprehension can be attributed to the speaker's concern about himself and the impression he is creating on his audience. It is natural for a person to want to make the best possible impression at all times. As a public speaker you are in a particularly vulnerable spot. You look at your audience and realize that all eyes are focused

[1]Floyd I. Greenleaf, "An Exploratory Study of Stagefright," *Quarterly Journal of Speech* 38 (1952): 326–30.

[2]Louis Lerue, "A Preliminary Study of the Verbal Behavior of Speech Fright," *Speech Monographs* 23 (1965): 229–33.

on you and, for a short time, at least, you are the main attraction. No one is going to stop you, no one is going to question you until you are finished speaking.

Another cause of communication apprehension, which is linked to the one previously discussed, is the speaker's concern about his topic. Is the topic appropriate for the assignment? Is it appropriate for this audience? Are the ideas organized so the audience can readily grasp them?

Beginning speakers sometimes are bothered by their *lack of experience*—but as in other learned skills, improvement can only be brought about through practice. You will find that most of your classmates are at approximately the same level of accomplishment.

There is no magic solution to the problem of stage fright. There are several things the speaker can do to help ease the problem. Most of these suggestions would be useful for general speech improvement in addition to helping develop self-confidence.

Careful, thorough preparation of the speech before the actual delivery of it for the audience is most wise. Most of your assignments will allow you ample time to prepare your speech. It is generally *best to spend a few minutes a day over several days rather than waiting until the night before the speech is due and preparing all of it.* Allow yourself time to narrow your topic and outline it clearly in your mind and perhaps discuss possible approaches to it with people who could help you.

One of the causes of communication apprehension is the concern of the speaker for herself—what impression is she making on her audience? As you gain experience as a speaker *concentrate more on your audience and less on yourself.* Concern yourself with the matter of communicating an idea. Watch the audience for signs of positive feedback. Generally, a receptive audience is an attentive one. Work to keep your listeners interested in what you are saying to them. Signs of boredom usually indicate the speaker is not living up to the audience's expectations of her.

Another thing you can do to develop more self-confidence is *to speak often.* Take advantage of opportunities to speak to different groups. After speaking to a group, analyze your effectiveness as a speaker. Explore in your mind the causes of any particular problems you are experiencing with delivery—attack one problem at a time until you are satisfied that you are doing your best.

Concentrate on slowing down and communicating ideas with your audience. Although individual words are important, they are merely vehicles for conveying an idea. As you begin to speak at a slower rate, you will begin to use greater variety of pitch and volume to help convey ideas.

Part II: Audience Attention

In his article dealing with life in Kentucky, Joe Creason, of the Louisville *Courier-Journal,* reported the following anecdote:

> . . . *reminds me of the farmer who was going to show a friend how to train a balky mule. They walked to the barn lot and the first thing the trainer did was pick up a 2 by 4 and break it over the mule's head.*
>
> *"First thing you got to do," he explained, "is get his attention."*[3]

Speech audiences aren't like mules in most respects, but the first thing you have to do in many public speeches is get the listeners' attention. Audience members subconsciously test an unfamiliar speaker for the first thirty seconds to two minutes. If the speech promises to be uninteresting, their attention soon begins to lose its focus. Once the speaker has lost initial audience attention, it is extremely difficult for him to regain it.

Control Whatever You Can

Certain aspects of audience attention are largely beyond the speaker's control. Such factors as listener motivation, expec-

[3]Joe Creason, "Joe Creason's Kentucky," Louisville *Courier-Journal,* July 16, 1968.

tancy, and habit[4] can be controlled to a limited extent by the speaker, but are primarily manipulated within the individual audience members.

However, the speaker can control many factors in gaining and maintaining listener attention. These are time-tested methods, and the wise speaker will select and use those most appropriate for his particular audience and speech occasion. The speaker who is unsuccessful at seizing and holding his listeners' attention will most assuredly fail in his overall purpose of informing or persuading those listeners.

Internal Attention Devices

Some of the most powerful means for focusing audience attention on the speaker and his subject are devices that can be made a part of the speech itself—internal attention devices. These are often used at the very beginning of a speech since gaining initial attention is such an important part of a successful speech. However, since they may also be found at any point after the introduction, they frequently serve to maintain attention once it has been established.

Narrative

Nearly everyone listens to a story, so the speaker who begins with one is almost assured of his listeners' attention until they hear the outcome. By the time the narrative is finished (even if it lasts for only a moment) most audiences have focused their attention on the speaker and are waiting to hear more. Of course, the best kind of story is one that has some natural connection with your speech topic. The following speech introduction illustrates how narrative can be used effectively:

> *We stand in a crowd of men and women—no children. Before*
> *us stretches a vast plain dotted with hundreds of animals*

[4]For a fuller discussion of these factors of attention, see Martin P. Andersen, Wesley Lewis, and James Murray, *The Speaker and His Audience* (New York: Harper & Row, Publishers, 1964), pp. 120–22.

innocently sleeping or moving lazily about. A group of men enters the scene and herds the brown fur together. Then another group appears; all are carrying clubs. As the spectators watch, these men mercilessly beat the calves, crushing their skulls. Some of the onlookers turn their heads trying to ignore the cries of the animals; others stare in a hypnotized horror; while a few nervously laugh at the grotesque struggle of those not quite dead.[5]

This disturbing narrative-description opened a speech dealing with the problem of the world's vanishing species. Undoubtedly, its story quality instantly engaged listener attention. Because the narrative was closely tied to the speaker's topic, it also served the secondary function of building audience interest in her subject. By the end of her introduction Miss John undoubtedly had each audience member listening intently for what was coming next.

Suspense

A similar kind of attention-getting introduction is the use of suspense. By withholding your theme or speech topic from your audience when you start, you can often create an atmosphere of expectancy that generates attention. Notice how a student speaker built suspense in this introduction:

Many years ago De Tocqueville, a French historian and political scientist, came to this country in the hopes of finding the source of America's greatness and genius. Upon returning to his native shores he wrote, "I sought for the greatness and genius of America in her commodious harbors and ample rivers, and it was not there. I sought for the greatness and genius of America in her fertile fields and boundless forests and it was not there. I sought for the greatness and genius of America in her rich mines and vast world commerce and it was not there. I sought for the greatness and genius of

[5]Deborah John, "Another Heaven . . . Another Earth," Speech given at the Interstate Oratorical Contest, May 5, 1972, Bowling Green, Kentucky.

America in her democratic Congress and her matchless Constitution and it was not there."

It was not until De Tocqueville, himself, went into the churches of America and heard pulpits flame with righteousness did he finally understand the secret of her genius and power. He realized that our America is great because our America is good and if our America ever ceases to be good, our America will cease to be great.[6]

The effect on the audience of this kind of introduction is to cause listeners to ask themselves, "If he did not find America's greatness there, then where?" Because the desire to answer the question grows within the listeners, their attention is being focused on the speaker and his topic.

A speaker should not try to hide his topic from his audience for too long a period of time. The amount of suspense utilized above is probably about right for most speeches.

Humor

Humor is one of the attention devices most widely and successfully used in public speaking. The speaker who can relate a funny incident or humorous anecdote and effect laughter among the listeners has usually succeeded in capturing audience attention. Several cautions relating to the use of humor in public speaking should be noted, however: (1) Do not use humor unless you have the ability to use it effectively. Some people have developed the knack of humorous storytelling and others have not. If you are not adept at arousing laughter among friends and acquaintances in private conversation, you should not attempt it in public speaking until you acquire the ability. When a speaker attempts to make his listeners laugh, and fails, the effect on his self-confidence and enthusiasm is usually negative. Be fairly sure of success before attempting humor in front of an audience. (2) If you are effective in the

[6]Jean Ansay, "The Season of Challenge," Speech given at the Interstate Oratorical Contest, May 5, 1972, Bowling Green, Kentucky.

use of humor, *do not overuse it.* Some speakers, who are very skillful at securing laughter from an audience, give in to the strong temptation to do little else. Consider humor in a speech to be similar to a spice for food—a little pepper on an egg can make it very tasty, but if the top comes off the pepper shaker and three or four teaspoons of pepper fall on the egg, it's overspiced and tastes very unpleasant. Humor in public speaking is a strong spice and should not be overused. Usually, one or two humorous anecdotes at the beginning of a speech, and one or two sprinkled throughout are sufficient. (3) Try to tie your humor to your speech topic. If you are going to speak on the credibility gap in government, you might start with a comment such as: "When you tell a man there are over 300 billion stars in the universe, he'll believe you. But if you tell him that a park bench has wet paint on it, he has to touch it to be sure." Because an opening like this relates to the matter of credibility, you can easily tie it to your speech topic. (4) Avoid the off-color joke. Your audience may laugh at this kind of humor, but your gains in the area of audience relaxation will usually be more than offset by your losses in prestige.[7] Your character in the eyes of your listeners is one of your most potent tools—keep it clean.

Common Ground

Probably the most frequently used attention device in public speaking is what is known as the "common ground" technique. The speaker begins by identifying experiences, careers, hobbies, interests, and preferences that she and her listeners share or have shared. She notes similarities that she and her audience possess in political or religious background, place of birth, ethnic heritage, or interest in certain sports—anything that highlights the fact that she and her listeners are alike in some respect. When Princess Margaret of the United Kingdom visited the Kentucky Derby and was asked to present a cup to the owner of the winning thoroughbred, she began her presentation speech by recalling the similarity between the Kentucky

---

[7]See Chapter 8 for a treatment of speaker ethos.

Derby and the English Derby. By doing this, she deemphasized her uniqueness as a princess from a foreign country and highlighted the interest in racing that she shared with her audience. This kind of "recognition of sameness" between speaker and listeners is an often-used method for assuring audience attention.

Naturally, the common ground technique is most effective when the similarities between speaker and listeners are great. If there is little that is really common to both to which the speaker can honestly refer, she would be wise to choose another attention device. Notice how effectively Larry Kay, a college student, utilized the common ground technique when his audience was mainly composed of other college students:

> *My name is Larry Kay, and I suppose I'm just like every other 18-year-old college student because I categorize things according to what I like to do and what I don't like to do. I consider such things as doing term papers, taking final examinations and waiting in line at 6:00 in the morning for class registration as 'Just Not My Bag' and yet I consider such things as fraternity parties, A's on my report cards, and summer vacation as 'Doing My Thing.'* [8]

Experiences like "doing term papers," and "fraternity parties" are the type that many of Larry's listeners had also experienced. Therefore, he undoubtedly seized his audience's attention from the start of his speech.

For a speaker to imply that he has had certain experiences which he actually has not had in order to establish common ground is not only a dangerous practice—it is also unethical. If a politician, for example, tells a rural audience that he was raised on a farm when, in reality, he grew up in suburban Chicago, he is lying to his listeners. This technique is called the "plainfolks device" rather than "common ground technique" and is a form of dishonest public speaking.

[8]Laurence Kay, "Marybeth, Casey, and Joe," Speech given at the Interstate Oratorical Contest, May, 1970, West Yellowstone, Montana.

Shock Technique

We live in a fast age—an age of supersonic jets, Telestar communications, and instant oatmeal. We like our speakers to move along quickly also—to develop their theme, give us a solution, and sit down. Thus, speakers will sometimes use the shock technique to demand instant audience attention. By mentioning an unusual, frightening, or almost unbelievable fact or statistic at the very beginning of a speech, a speaker can often "shock" his listeners to instant attention. The speaker who begins an anti-abortion speech by saying: "It was announced this week by the Bureau of Census that there were more legal abortions than births in Washington, D.C. last year" is almost guaranteed the immediate attention of her listeners. Naturally, such a speaker must have factual backing for making such a statement.

Notice how a student speaker made good use of the shock technique to assure audience attention from the first sentence of his address:

> *If I were to tell you that there are 3.6 billion people on the earth, with more arriving at the rate of 132 per minute, these figures would probably do nothing more than bore you. If, on the other hand, I were to say 'There's a bomb in this room and it could explode at any second!!!' it is likely that I would have your attention, and you would realize the urgency in what I had said. The cold facts, however, are that the bomb I warned you about and the figures I cited are actually one and the same thing. That bomb is known as the Population Bomb, and it is ticking right now in this room and all over the world.*[9]

Not only did the shocking statistics demand the immediate attention of this speaker's audience, their subject matter provided a natural lead into his topic, which dealt with over-

[9]Thom Mayer, "The Population Bomb," Speech given at the Interstate Oratorical Contest, May, 1971, Omaha, Nebraska.

population. As with the use of humor, the shocking facts or statistics used to gain attention should also have a natural connection with the main theme of the speech.

Repetition

Because spoken language, unlike that which is written, often must be understood quickly or not at all by listeners, speakers have traditionally repeated their material more than have writers. Saying the same word or series of words over several times not only seems to firmly implant the material in the listener's memory, but also generates attention in an audience. Thus, it often happens that a speaker utilizes repetition in a speech at the point at which audience interest and attention need to be at their highest. Martin Luther King, Jr.'s well-known repetition of "I have a dream" is an excellent example of this psychological use of repetition. The conclusion of a speech is often a critical point at which repetition is used to regenerate flagging attention and to effect a lasting impression upon the memory of the audience. The conclusion of a speech against abortion illustrates this dual use of repetition:

> *The abortion advocate would have you believe that the fetus is nonhuman. But I have shown you that he is human. . . . The abortion advocate would have you believe the fetus has no legal rights. But I have shown you that the law is concerned with the potential humanity of the fetus, and upholds his human rights on condition of his birth. . . . The abortion advocate would have you believe that abortion is socially necessary. But I have shown you it only turns matters of life and death into matters of convenience and inconvenience.*[10]

Other Attention Devices

The preceding list of ways by which a speaker can generate audience attention is not a complete list. Narrative, suspense,

[10]Virginia Coom, "Let There Be Life," Speech given at the Interstate Oratorical Contest, May, 1971, Omaha, Nebraska.

humor, common ground, shock technique, and repetition are probably the most commonly used attention devices, but there are others, often more applicable to a particular audience, speech occasion, or speaker's personality:

1. The *rhetorical question* can generate rapid attention at the beginning of a speech—"What would you do with one hundred thousand dollars?"
2. *Contrast*—that is, the use of balanced ideas and sentence structures—will usually demand audience attention: "Ask not what your country can do for you—ask what you can do for your country."
3. References to what is *familiar* to your listeners, such as mentioning the name of their hometown or a T.V. commercial that is well known, is an effective means of re-generating flagging attention among your audience.

Besides these internal devices, devices that are contained within the structure of the speech itself, several external factors can likewise have a considerable influence on how much listener attention will be focused on the speaker. Factors such as the temperature, ventilation, and lighting in the listening area should be carefully checked before the speech begins, as should the microphone and the audience seating arrangements. All of these can have a considerable effect on the outcome of the speech. If any or all of them are not conducive to comfortable listening and viewing, an otherwise excellent speech can fail to capture the center of audience attention. The wise speaker will arrive early to check carefully these external attention factors.

Summary

Most speakers encounter a problem with lack of self-confidence. Although there is no one universal solution to this problem, several things can be done to help the speaker overcome the problem. The speaker should prepare thoroughly.

He should focus his attention upon his audience instead of himself. He can speak often and slow down.

Audience attention may be gained and maintained by using a number of time-tested devices, each of which is designed to focus the center of the listener's attention on the speaker and the message. Probably the most commonly used attention devices are narrative, suspense, humor, common ground, shock technique, and repetition. The rhetorical question, use of contrast, and reference to the familiar are perhaps less commonly used, but very effective when used appropriately.

Several factors, external to the speech itself, relate to audience attention: room temperature, ventilation and lighting, the microphone, and audience seating arrangements. Careful checking of these factors for audience comfort before the speech begins can help assure close attention to your presentation.

EXERCISES ❧

1. Analyze an experienced speaker you have heard recently in terms of self-confidence.

2. Write a paper describing how stage fright affects you. In this paper analyze what you consider to be the causes for your stage fright.

3. Interview someone who speaks frequently before groups. Have this person share any suggestions he or she has for developing confidence as a speaker.

4. Keep a diary in this class in which you indicate your feelings before and after giving successive speeches.

5. Complete the Gilkinson Personal Report on Confidence as a Speaker found in Appendix B and give it to your instructor. The instructor may wish an individual conference with you if responses indicate a conference is needed.

Organizing and Outlining the Speech*

*By Carl Kell.

OBJECTIVES ❧

After completing this chapter, you should be able to:

1. *Discover* appropriate speech subjects for the classroom experience.
2. *Discover* a variety of speech topics within each subject you select.
3. *Locate* appropriate supporting material for your speech.
4. *Select* an appropriate theme for your speech and arrange an appropriate organizational pattern for the body of the speech.
5. *Construct* an appropriate introduction and conclusion for the speech.
6. *Construct* a speech outline for a variety of in-class and/or out-of-class exercises.

As in the creation of other art forms (music, painting, or poetry), speech communication requires a sense of, and for, creative thought, order, and balance. In this chapter, you will be guided through a series of techniques, rules, and advice about "public" speech communication. Our specific intent is to provide a step-by-step organizational system for effective public speaking.

By and large, this chapter will be concerned with *you*, the student, as a speech communicator in the "captive audience" situation of the classroom. In a real sense, your audience comprises the students in your class who, on any given speech assignment "day," constitute your *real* audience. To learn how to select, prepare, and adapt a speech for their benefit is the real challenge of your first course in speech communication.

Selecting a Topic

Perhaps the most frustrating feeling that the beginning speech student can have is when the instructor gives the first assignment in broad terms such as, "You may speak on any topic you wish for five minutes." With this announcement panic quickly overcomes the student who suddenly realizes that no topic seems appropriate and five minutes seems like five hours. Typically, this initial assignment will allow you only several days of preparation time at best, so you must plunge into your work. Outside of the classroom, speakers are frequently requested to make a speech about "something" without the inviting party carefully identifying the topic. Therefore, this process of "start-up" has usefulness outside the classroom.

If your topic area is completely open, try to list indiscriminately a variety of current events topics dealing with social, political, or moral questions. Your first effort should be to make a list of as many possible general topics as you can develop. It is important for you to list all topics that come to mind if they seem vaguely applicable. Your first reaction should not be critical; you will have plenty of time to go back and criticize your spontaneous list. This operation is typically referred to as *brainstorming,* and it is a crucial first step in the development of a speech.

Once you have a sizeable list developed, begin to review the list in a critical manner eliminating topics if: (1) they seem unsuited to the audience; (2) you feel uncomfortable with the topic; (3) you are not motivated by the topic; (4) you are concerned that the topic will be "overworked" by other members of the class; or (5) you are concerned that you will be unable to find sufficient information on the topic. Occasionally a student is too critical in reviewing a brainstormed list and will eliminate all of the potential topics. Obviously, you should make careful judgments but avoid being too easily convinced against a topic.

In working through topics to arrive at your final choice, it may be possible to combine some of the topics that were listed in the brainstorming process, or some of these original topic ideas may serve as subpoints under the final topic selected.

In selecting a possible speech subject, review your personal interests and those interests you perceive in your class audience. Campus, local, state, and national issues that affect you usually affect the people around you, those people in *your* class. Are you interested in college basketball? Do you watch your school's team as an avid fan? If so, you may be aware of the new rules for the National Collegiate Athletic Association that affect spectator response and critical appreciation. A speech to inform on the new rules, with a visual demonstration of the differences between the old and new rules would probably be appreciated by virtually every member of your class. A speech to persuade on the same subject area might not be appreciated by the class because they couldn't actually *change* or approve the rules of the NCAA. Review your interests and those of your class. Examine your school newspaper, campus organizations, university-community affairs, and national affairs to discover subjects that your class already has an interest in and would appreciate knowing more about. At the same time, be sensitive to subjects along these same lines that your class audience cares *little* about or could *do* little about.

Here are some examples of speech ideas of class interest that could be used for informative or persuasive formats:

1. Student parking on campus
   a. To inform: a discussion of new campus parking plans to add to and change existing areas.
   b. To persuade: a series of proposals you support for greater flexibility in campus parking.
2. Registration for university classes
   a. To inform: a discussion of the university's policies and procedures for registration as they presently exist.

    b. To persuade: a discussion of new proposals for a more effective process of registration than now exists under the present system.

3. A city (or university) beautification project

    a. To inform: a discussion of proposals under way to beautify and alter the landscape of your university community's main business sector.

    b. To persuade: a discussion of support for or rejection of the city's proposals and the substitution of a new proposal or appeal to retain the status quo.

It should be obvious by now that the easiest speech ideas come from the day-by-day concerns of every young person in college. However, many issues or subjects can affect students' lives, but because these subjects aren't constantly in the front page of the newspaper or aren't the number one topic at bull sessions, they get little attention from the beginning speech communicator. We will be discussing research for the speech subject in Chapter 8, but here are some ideas on the potentially *good* speech idea, using either an informative or a persuasive format:

1. Student retention in the 1970s

    a. To inform: a discussion about the causes of decreased student enrollment across the country and particularly in the speaker's school or regional area.

    b. To persuade: to recommend action proposals for greater student retention in the speaker's school or regional area.

2. The nature and types of national academic tests: for example, LSAT, Graduate Record Exam, ACT.

    a. To inform: to inform the class about the various kinds of tests that indicate a student's preparedness for career or vocational life styles.

    b. To persuade: to reveal the valid weaknesses of certain national tests and to argue for greater personal development through rigorous college or vocational programs.

3. College students and the game of politics
    a. To inform: describe and detail the local and/or state campus political organizations and their past and present roles in the political systems of the state and national parties.
    b. To persuade: to alter the common student premises of "apathy" concerning politics (the "Watergate" syndrome) by calling for a personal commitment to political activity to improve the political fortunes of the state or national two-party system.

Remember, the choice of subject should be made after analyzing your class as members of a *specific* group of people or as members of college-aged young people not unlike thousands across the country.

Whatever you can do to make yourself more believable as an authority will pay off for you in your success as a speaker. Some general guidelines of helpful ways of increasing your believability are:

1. Conduct yourself physically in a manner appropriate to the setting and occasion.
2. Demonstrate your grasp of the issues by indicating your personal experience or the extent of your research.
3. Demonstrate your fairness in examining all sides of the question.
4. Show respect for alternate points of view.
5. Indicate the motivation for your position on the issue.

These same considerations should be made by each member of the audience to be an effective listener.

Locating Supporting Material

Even a beginning speech student can easily answer the question of where to locate supporting material with the obvious answer "in the library!" If only the problem were that simple, we could delete the following section. The typical speech student, however, will find his or her job much more difficult and will appreciate the following elaboration on where to locate and how to go about obtaining the supporting material discussed above. In general it is important for the beginning student to research material from general background information first, then seek out the far more specific information which will be required to substantiate certain points within a speech. Quite frequently students will respond to the question, "Where would you go for the first source of information on a speech?" with the response, "I would check the *Readers Guide to Periodical Literature* for a good up-to-date magazine article." While this source of information is an extremely valuable one, it is not always the place to begin researching a topic. The speaker should first take stock of the knowledge which he already possesses on the topic. Occasionally he will already be well versed in general on a topic and general background reading will not be necessary. More likely, however, a speaker should begin research on a speech topic with a general study of background information. This can easily be done through reading an encyclopedia article. Keep in mind that there are many types of encyclopedias and the student should not automatically go immediately to the *Encyclopaedia Britannica.* You should ascertain which encyclopedia will deal most directly with the general topic being researched. If you are in doubt about this, consult your reference librarian about your general topic area and ask for help in ascertaining which encyclopedia will give you the best general background of your topic. Use the encyclopedia for gaining a broad general understanding and not for specific support. It is rarely acceptable to refer to an encyclopedia in your speech as a direct quotable source.

The next general source of information to which you should go is the card catalog to locate books on the subject. The card catalog subject index is the appropriate place to locate general reading on the broad topical subject. Again, keep in mind that at this point in your preparation you should be looking for general information to give you the broad background. A book can give breadth as well as the specific supporting material which can be used directly in the speech, whereas an encyclopedia would not be used as specific supporting material but only for background information. One difficulty with using books is their volume and the amount of time which will be consumed by reading the entire book. A student must make a judgment as to how much time can be placed into researching the background information on a general topic. The encyclopedia will present a broad general background briefly and most articles in the encyclopedia can be read easily in one sitting.

After consulting these kinds of general references for the broad background of a topic, the student is now ready to pursue more specific types of information and is ready to consult the *Readers Guide to Periodical Literature* for general interest magazines and journals. The *Readers Guide to Periodical Literature* is a reference index of general news and pleasure reading magazines. You can locate with the *Guide* the general subject index that covers your topic. It will also provide for you a listing of articles which deal with this particular topic, including the volume number, the date of publication, and the pages on which the article can be found.

If your topic lends itself to articles published in professional and scholarly journals, then you should look in the *Education Index*, as well as *Readers Guide to Periodical Literature*. The *Education Index* is similar to the *Guide* in that it is an indexing and reference item showing articles on specific topical issues. Again, look for a general topical heading which corresponds as closely as possible with the general topic of the speech you are considering. After locating this general topical heading in the *Education Index* you will find listed a series of scholarly and professional journals and articles dealing with your topic. The listing will show the title of the article, the journal in which the article appeared, and all other necessary information for you to locate that article.

In addition to this type of specific information, you might also find a number of special documents available in the library. Government publications, for instance, can be an invaluable source of information for the student speaker. Government documents are usually housed in a separate area of the library and often have a special librarian to serve as an assistant in locating relevant materials. If you believe that your topic is on an issue of public importance, so that government agencies might have been involved in making a detailed study or analysis (or providing a congressional report on the topic), then you will probably find a specific government document which could be of great help to you. In addition to government documents, other specific resource items are frequently available in college libraries. Consult the reference librarian for other specific documents which might be available in the library.

If you have sufficient time to prepare for your topic prior to giving a speech, you might find it valuable to write to various public or private agencies involved in the issue on which you are speaking. For instance, in a speech on the hazards of cancer, you could obtain valuable information from the local American Cancer Society office. A student speaking on drug addiction would find various local health agencies anxious to provide material dealing with drug problems. Use your imagination to locate areas of special interest and special expertise in your community from which you would be able to obtain additional specific information.

If sufficient time is available, you might also consider writing personal letters to authorities on your specific subject. Students will frequently find a letter to a member of Congress helpful and stimulating in preparing for their speeches. Other public officials in various elected offices as well as people in private life are usually anxious to help a student who is searching on a problem and who demonstrates genuine interest and concern about the issue. If you word your letter tactfully and indicate your genuine interest in the topic, you will usually get a very positive and helpful response. This requires time, however, and you must allow several weeks to obtain a response if you attempt to write personal letters.

One other way to obtain specific information is the personal interview. This can be accomplished either through telephone calls in which you discuss your issue with a knowledgeable person on the campus or in the local community, or through arranging a personal appointment in the office of the person you wish to interview. People in a university community and people in most public offices are happy to discuss the issues and their positions with a student who has a genuine interest. Pursue a telephone call or a personal interview tactfully and you can find this a personally rewarding experience as well as helpful in the preparation of your speech.

Retrieving and Recording Information

Researching for a speech is hard work and involves a kind of careful systematic effort which few students will cheerfully give. Experience shows, however, that a few minutes of extra effort and a little special attention to detail can pay off significantly when you begin to put the speech together. Students will typically go to the library to research for a speech and simply take down notes at random in a regular notebook on regular paper and without consideration for any system. Typically, a student will simply record information—statistics, quotations, specific examples, illustrations, and anecdotes collected at random throughout a set of notes in a notebook. In terms of recording the information, this presents no problem. The information is recorded and is retrievable, but at great difficulty and with great loss of time. If you follow this plan, you will find yourself searching for that piece of information that you remember recording but which became lost in your mass of notes. That is why a little special attention and a little extra time in the recording of information will prove to be such a valuable system when a student attempts to retrieve the information.

Although it may take a few more minutes in recording information if you do it in a systematic way, this method will prove invaluable as you retrieve the material and will make the information much easier to use. If you appropriately record your information in a systematic way, it is much easier for you to sort that information and relate it to the subpoints which you are attempting to support as you develop your speech. The most recognized way of systematically recording material is to use a note card approximately 4 by 6 inches. A 3 by 5 inch card appears quite small and will not hold very much information, and a 5 by 8 inch card is fairly large and is less manageable in the same sense that an 8½ by 11 inch piece of paper is less manageable. Also, a note card is preferable to paper because it is less flimsy and less likely to be lost in the shuffle. In recording your material, in either the upper left or upper right hand corner of the note card, identify the subject index and give a broad general heading as well as a subheading to the item of information being recorded. Follow this with a complete statement of reference indicating where the material was found. Then proceed with the recording of the actual information (see Figure 3.1).

When making decisions about "should or should I not record this piece of information?" accept as a general rule that you should always decide in favor of recording as much information as possible. It is easier to file away unused material than to make an extra trip back to the library to hunt for a piece of supporting material which you remember reading in some area of your research. If you have already tentatively determined

MAJOR TOPICAL HEADING

Author's name, "Title of Article,"
Source of Publication, page numbers.
(Use any standard bibliographic entry form.)

Copy your supporting notes in this area. Use the
back side of the card or additional cards
if necessary.

Figure 3.1

the subpoints of your speech, you can use these subpoints as the subject indexes at the top of the note cards. After you have collected all of your data and have begun to develop and build the speech, it is relatively easy to sort out the supporting material and relate and identify it with the subpoints of your speech. At this stage you will be able to review more carefully the material which was recorded and isolate more specifically that portion of the material which you want to directly quote or use in developing the substance of your speech.

Selecting and Arranging the Topic

The next obligation in preparing a speech is to know exactly what the purpose will be in the speech situation. Whether the class assignment is informative or persuasive, a clearly stated purpose is essential. In the *informative* situation, you should phrase a declarative sentence that accomplishes two important points—a *transitional* phrase to tell the audience that this sentence *is* the speech purpose sentence and then the *actual speech purpose clause* itself. For example:

> *"For the next few moments, I will discuss the legal concept of 'Nolo contendere' used by former Vice President Spiro Agnew during his last days in public office."*
>
> *"This afternoon, the purpose of my speech will be to shed light on the NCAA College Division Playoff System in intercollegiate football."*
>
> *"With our college graduation just around the corner, I will present the shocking truth about the job market in the late 1970s."*

In the *persuasive* situation, the same general phrasing procedure should also be used. For example:

> *"This morning, I will propose two equally workable remedies to the parking problem on our campus."*

"My answer to the serious issue of campus rape is a series of suggestions offered by the City Police."

"Today, I will outline the official Red Cross procedures for administering emergency first aid to a swimming accident victim."

A cardinal rule of speech organization is that the speech purpose should clearly rule the entire direction of the speech and the main points should clearly support and explain the speech purpose. A key problem for most students is that they confuse the concept of main points and speech purpose. For example:

Wrong: Today, I want to examine the campus water drainage problems at the corner of Jones and Smith Avenue, etc. . . .

Right: This afternoon, I am going to examine the water drainage problem on our campus by discussing three critical problem areas:
1. The corner of Jones and Smith Avenue.
2. The University "X" parking lot.
3. The Parking Garage at University and Parker Avenue.

Each speech must have a stated direction that can be accomplished in some suitable fashion as well as within the classroom-assigned time limit. Phrasing a speech purpose consisting only of main points gives no real direction to your speech. Regardless of the speech assignment, informative or persuasive, the listener needs to have a clear picture as to the difference between the purpose of your speech and the supporting main points that detail and explain the speech purpose.

Several organizational patterns exist which present the speech purpose and develop appropriate main points. The most common patterns are:

1. Chronological
2. Spatial
3. Topical
4. Problem-solution

Just as patterns for organizing a speech are recognized, certain speaker-audience rules should be followed. First, always allow the particular speech purpose to dictate the type of organizational pattern the speech will follow. For example, to persuade your audience that "the state should adopt a no-fault car insurance system," any of the above patterns might be useful as organizational approaches. However, one type will eventually emerge as the *best* form based on the available research. It is suggested here that either a topical or a problem-solution approach would fit a persuasive speech advocating a policy of no-fault car insurance.

Second, the speaker should *never* impose an organizational pattern upon a speech purpose just to use that particular pattern. Such an organizational effort violates the "real world" situation of public speakers adapting their knowledge of their subject and then adapting their subject and pattern of presentation to their audience.

The organizational patterns listed above for speech preparation serve different ends:

1. CHRONOLOGICAL   Perhaps a discussion of time or historical events is most appropriate in presenting your chosen speech topic. For example:

> *This morning, we are honoring the man who founded the John Smith Memorial Stadium. His years of service to our University are worthy of review and public appreciation. For the next few minutes, we will honor President Smith as:*
> *Dean of Men of the University: 1926–50.*
> *Dean of Students of the University: 1951–65 and President of the University: 1966–77.*

When using the *chronological* pattern to highlight a span of time or a sweep of history, remember that the pattern is intended to encompass a set of experiences or events. The chronological pattern should start and finish an analysis in terms of time and/or dates.

2. SPATIAL   Quite often, a student may wish to describe, compare and contrast, or advocate an analysis that relates the

known to the unknown. When you inform a friend where the county court house is located, you draw word pictures relating streets or buildings that the person may know to the place he is trying to find. Similarly, in an analysis in which you are trying to do somewhat the same thing, you would use a spatial pattern of speech organization. For instance:

> *For the next few minutes, I am going to discuss the new downtown mall concept by explaining:*
> *Phase I—The demolition and rebuilding of the streets and shops North of the city square.*
> *Phase II—The remodeling of the streets and shops South of the city square.*
> *Phase III—The closing of the one-way streets East and West of the city square.*
> *Phase IV—The completion of the entire project by 1979.*

3. TOPICAL   It is easier to explain the ways that a topical analysis might be used than perhaps any other organizational form. It may be best to consider using an analysis of various "topics" suggested by your speech purpose when you wish to cover an unusually large number of ideas in a brief period of time.

> *Today, we are going to examine the traits of teamwork in our organization.*
> *Selflessness*
> *Courage*
> *Integrity*
> *Pride*

Any set of functions, rules, procedures, steps in a plan for action, strategies for a program, or almost any grouping of elements that together explain a *whole* concept, might best be served by using the topical outline.

4. PROBLEM-SOLUTION   The key point to remember in using this organizational approach is that you are reasonably sure that the "solution" is strong enough medicine to handle

the "problem" you wish to discuss. By now, you should be getting the hang of these examples of the various organizational formats. However, let's try this one on the problem-solution organizational mode.

> *In the midst of the energy crisis and our cities' response to our energy needs, I am going to outline seven basic action proposals that you can be doing to conserve energy. They are:*
> *Electrical considerations in the home.*
> *Gasoline consumption.*
> *Tire care.*
> *Water utilization.*
> *Car pools for business and industry.*
> *Home improvements.*
> *Heating and cooling the home.*

We have examined briefly the most commonly used organizational models of speech organization. Your instructor may extend the development of these concepts as well as provide you with other alternatives and examples. The most important aspect to remember is that you should maintain one organizational pattern throughout the body of your speech. Do *not* mix the patterns of organization within the body of your speech. Remember, your speaker obligation is to discover the most appropriate mode of speech organization and then to word it so that the speech flows smoothly for maximum listener comprehension.

Introducing and Concluding the Speech

What has been stressed so far is the manner in which a speech, informative or persuasive, should be *prepared* rather than *delivered.* In keeping with this sequence, let us now turn to the next major step in speech preparation—the introduction and conclusion.

Even in the speech classroom (laboratory) situation, you can select and adapt speech materials to your audience, polish and perfect them, and present them on your audience's language level. First, you have a ready storehouse of "introductory" materials within the particular speech subject you have chosen to present. For example, you might select a humorous incident within the speech topic; a set of facts pinpointing the problem, interest value, or entertainment quality of the speech topic; a humorous story, allegory, analogy, or any other figure of speech which captures the audience's attention and interest.

A rule of introduction-planning is to select the best language tool(s) which captures the attention and the interest of the audience on the speech topic as quickly and concretely as possible. Choice is an important communication technique in planning the introduction, so plan carefully *which* speech element does the best job for you. The introduction must be brief, well worded, and topic-related to capture and sustain the audience's initial inclination to "tune you out" early in the speech. Quite often, your first remarks are the most important ones of the entire speech. Far too often the beginning student speaker is inclined to simply say, "Hello, I'd like to talk to you today about a subject you should know something about, etc. . . . ." There's no imagination or flair in such an opening statement and your classmates or any audience is likely to say silently "who cares?" *You* must care about the introduction because your speaker responsibility is to either inform, persuade, or perhaps entertain your audience for a prescribed amount of time. So, don't take the introduction lightly.

The introduction of your speech should generally comprise the following elements:

1. An attention-getting device.
2. A subject-related series of comments that introduces the topic to be shared.
3. A purpose sentence which "tells" the audience, with some degree of precision, what the speaker has chosen to discuss specifically about the topic.
4. A preview of the major headings of the speech.

For example:

> *In yesterday's campus paper, it was announced that the university had established a freshman-sophomore residency requirement to be initiated this fall. In the face of rising costs, we were all aware of the inevitability of such a move. This morning, I am not so concerned with why such a decision was made as with how our student body is going to live with the decision.*
>
> *With that knotty problem in mind, I'd like to discuss the greater concern of 'the quality of student life' under the new mandatory dorm policy. To accomplish my purpose, I will cover two major areas: (1) the negative and positive effects of 100 percent dorm occupancy, and (2) a new series of dorm policies to meet the students' needs for the 1970s.*

In any speech situation, the circumstances of speech type, nature of the audience, difficulty of material, and a host of other considerations help to determine the length, nature, and composition of a speech introduction and for that matter, the entire speech. Remember, the art of speech-making is bound up in discovering the available materials for speech composition in the research and audience end of the event we call a *public* speech. Organizing the speech introduction is a matter of selecting the most appropriate speech forms. So, be communicatively sensitive in these matters and you will find your speeches attaining a level of common ground directly related to your audience.

The purpose of a conclusion is genuinely to put an *end* to your speech. No one wants an untimely "death" for one's speech, and a well-developed conclusion can summarize the ideas of the speech, deliver a clinching appeal to your arguments, or save your best topic-related joke for the last. Obviously, the conclusion should convey a sense of direction which agrees with and naturally fulfills the direction established by the introduction. In the final position of the speech, the conclusion should pull together the major units of the speech in the same order as they were presented. A conclusion of the speech about mandatory freshman-sophomore dorm residency might be:

As you can see, we must live with and in the new mandatory dorm residency policy. It is hoped that we can also show and request a concern for "the quality of student life" in coming semesters. As I have attempted to argue, we must exhibit an awareness of first, the negative and positive effects of 100 percent dorm occupancy and, second, a search for new dorm policies to meet the students' needs for the late '70s.

Finally, let's "pitch in" and make the system work. The facts of a better student life for the first two years of college are in our favor. Let's not "blow it" by complaints and threats.

The speech below was delivered by a student speaker in a speech class and later at an interstate oratorical contest. As you read it, decide how well organized you consider it to be.

It Could Cost Too Much[1]

We picture the college athlete as the hero. He seems to be destined for future greatness. You can pick him out on any campus. His jacket bears a varsity letter. He is surrounded by coeds. He is the center of any group in the snack bar.

This is an illusion. Our minds are performing trickery, because the outlook for many athletes today is not quite so bright as the scene just pictured. Colleges and universities have succeeded in manufacturing athletes but have somehow neglected to qualify them for anything else. This year many young men will terminate their college athletic careers only to find themselves poorly equipped for life, almost totally unprepared to enter a vocation commensurate with their years of education.

Let me tell you a story. A friend of mine has been playing basketball for most of his life. John was an outstanding high school athlete and later a successful collegiate basketball performer. In fact, he did well enough to be drafted by the professional leagues but he failed to make the team. At present

---

[1]Steve Eaton, "It Could Cost Too Much." Speech given at the Interstate Oratorical Contest, May 5, 1962, Bowling Green, Kentucky.

John is unemployed, floating around the league trying to catch on with another team. Maybe John will finally make it as a professional, but that is not the point.

This young man is not by any means stupid. But in college he took just enough courses to remain eligible for competition. Roughly, this boiled down to twelve semester hours of attempted credit per semester. John did not graduate and is in no position to soon do so.

More important than John's attitude was the attitude of the university. His coaches gave him a wealth of advice about the least demanding courses and the best instructors to take in order to remain eligible. They even spread their influence when needed to obtain for him a passing grade. In the long run John was the loser. He attended college for four years but has little to show for it. In reality John's only purpose in attending college was to play basketball. Eligibility was only a necessary evil to be satisfied by putting forth as little effort as possible. Aside from basketball John is no more qualified to enter a vocation than any high school graduate. The university's professed interest was only a superficial one—its real interest was in John's athletic contributions, not his educational progress.

As an athlete in a major university program I have had occasion to know several fellow athletes and their situations. Two and a half years ago our basketball team elected captains. A young man whom we will call Jimmy was elected. To everyone's surprise he quit the team. He was severely criticized for being disloyal to the basketball team and ungrateful for what the school had done for him. This simply was not the case. Jimmy had been stereotyped as an athlete and wanted to establish a new identity. He desired that people know him as an individual, for he felt that athletics was only one aspect of his life. The point of this is not to proclaim Jimmy's action as a standard. It is only to illustrate that in numerous instances college athletic programs have lost their sense of direction. Athletic departments have become more than appendages to universities. They have become separate entities. Athletic departments often do nothing more than serve as training schools for future professional athletes.

There are two points which must be crystalized. First, a university cannot be blamed for every athlete's failure to obtain a college degree. Second, I can tell you from personal experience that there are coaches who are sincerely interested in the education of their athletes. Sadly enough, this latter condition does not seem to be the general trend.

At present there are over 750 colleges and universities affiliated with the NCAA, the National Collegiate Athletic Association. Almost 550 colleges and universities belong to the NAIA, the National Association of Intercollegiate Athletics. This number represents over 90 percent of four-year colleges in the United States, thus giving the problem at hand unquestioned relevance. University administrators need to stop and take a hard look at college athletics. What is the real purpose of athletics? What role should it play in the university? Does a university not have a moral responsibility to every student to provide an atmosphere in which a meaningful education can be pursued? Should not an athletic department blend with the broader goals of the university?

Athletic teams have traditionally been the pride of many universities. These teams have brought prestige of a sort and helped students and alumni identify with their schools. But the recent history of college sports points to the growing pressure on coaches to produce "winners." It seems that in order to be successful the football team must be victorious every Saturday. Visit with any coach and it will not take long to recognize that his primary concern is to produce a winning team. This in itself is not degrading but if it becomes the only goal of our athletic departments we receive some harmful radiation from the fallout. This attitude of "victory at all costs" has created several results.

One of the most visible features is the intense competition in recruiting. In order to be successful a coach must have the best material available. The day is long past when a college simply offers an athlete an opportunity to obtain his college degree in exchange for his participation in athletics. The athlete generally goes to the highest bidder. You remember John, my friend? During his senior year in high school he was actively recruited by several schools. Through personal pref-

erence he narrowed his choice to two. One school offered him five thousand dollars outright. The other school, although less specific, promised to show its gratitude.

Dave Meggyesy, in his recent book, Out of Their League, *has exposed a second result. It is a truism that many top college athletes have become semi-professional while still amateur. Meggyesy writes of his undergraduate days at Syracuse University where he was All-American football player. Most of the top players on that team received from ten to fifty dollars per week. In other words these were college athletes being paid to play football. The coaches usually gave the money in a handshake, but often they merely handed the players a brown envelope containing money. On one occasion, Meggyesy was attempting to put on his street shoe and could not understand what was causing the discomfort. He tipped it up and a crumpled twenty-dollar bill fell out.*

Incidents such as this are much to blame for the rise of an employer-employee relationship between coach and players. The athlete often looks on himself and his role in the school as that of employee. He has become the property of the university. The athlete is there, not to receive his education, but to perform.

A third result has been that academics have become a tool in remaining eligible. No effort is put forth to prepare the athlete to be other than a sports figure for the remainder of his life.

The main concern of coaches has become that of keeping their athletes eligible, not one of encouraging them to make progress toward a degree.

Perhaps the most disgusting aspect of all the de-emphasis placed on academics has been the various attempts to assist athletes in achieving their grades. Mr. Meggyesy has written about certain courses which were offered only to athletes at Syracuse University. Attendance was not required. They were in effect free grade courses since athletes received automatic "A's" simply by registering. If players needed extra hours of credit to remain eligible they could enroll for these special classes and at the end of the term receive six hours of "A" for unattended courses.

The athlete is a commodity to be used by the university and then disposed of. The minute his eligibility expires the athletic department's concern for his welfare suddenly evaporates. The free tutoring stops and an athlete finds himself faced with a flock of difficult classes.

Earlier this year the school board in Philadelphia announced the elimination of athletics in the city schools. An interesting sidelight to the controversy was the argument which went back and forth concerning the merits of athletics. One opinion raised was that the discontinuance of sports would deprive many city youths, especially poor blacks, of a college education. The Superintendent of City Schools replied by citing this statistic: three out of every four blacks who attend college on an athletic scholarship never receive their degree. Does this tell us something about the climate of college athletics?

All of the conditions described are but symptoms of the same disease—that is, an unhealthy overemphasis on winning. Jack Scott, Athletic Director at Oberlin College and author of The Athletic Revolution, *was quoted in the May 24, 1971 issue of* Time Magazine *as saying: "The process of sport is more important than the product. The beauty is in the classic struggle of man against man, man against nature and man against himself. The index of how well you do is how well you struggle." The final score should be almost incidental.*

Unfortunately this has not been the prevalent opinion in our colleges and universities. The pressure to win exerted by spectators, whether they be alumni, local community, or the school administration, has helped cloud the issue.

Where should we search for the solution?

If we are to reorder the priorities of college athletics who should exert the leadership? First, the impetus for action must be initiated by college and university administrations. Only they can provide the leadership necessary to make athletic departments a more homogeneous part of educational institutions. Many universities maintain million dollar sports budgets but still manage to operate in the red. This is but another indication of the lengths to which athletic depart-

ments feel compelled to go to produce winning teams. College administrators are capable of providing the counter-pressure needed to reduce this exorbitant spending.

Also, the role of the athlete needs redefinition. The athlete must be treated as a human being, not as a commodity owned by the university.

Recall the story of the young man who was selected captain of the basketball team and shortly thereafter quit. He wanted people to know him as a real person, not just as an athlete. This is the essence of much that I have said. It is past time for universities to recognize college athletes as students first and then as athletes.

Mr. Eaton's speech was given in the 1972 Interstate Oratorical Association competition. Since Mr. Eaton delivered the speech by memory, we can only guess as to the nature and form of his outline.

Summary

This chapter provided you with a step-by-step speech organizational system for effective public speaking. The first step is to choose an appropriate topic, whether your speech is to inform or to persuade. Examine your own interests and those of your audience. After you select a topic, you must develop a clearly stated purpose, which you maintain throughout the speech. Organizational patterns of a speech include: chronological, spatial, topical, and problem-solution. The last major step in your speech preparation is to formulate the introduction and conclusion. By no means have we provided you with all the answers. Rather, our specific attempt has been to provide the right questions with which to approach your speech class "audience" on the variety of assignments that you will be asked to complete. You will become more communicatively sensitive to the demands of the speaker-audience situation as you continually seek to make the better choices in your speech preparation. Your instructor will be your chief aid in honing your communication skills. Don't hesitate in seeking his or her counsel.

EXERCISES ᘓᕤᕽᕤ

1. Your instructor can provide you with an excellent simulation for learning the dimensions of speech composition. See Theodore Clevenger, Jr., "The Rhetorical Jigsaw Puzzle: A Device for Teaching Certain Aspects of Speech Composition," *Speech Teacher* 12, no. 2 (March, 1963): 114–46.

2. Construct a speech outline of "It Could Cost Too Much."

3. Devote a class period or more to organizing and outlining a variety of speeches on the blackboard with your instructor serving as a facilitator-leader and the entire class providing input.

Using Language Effectively*

4

*By Larry James Winn.

OBJECTIVES ⤳

After completing this chapter, you should be able to:

1. *Recognize* four traps of language and *identify* ways to avoid each.
2. *List* four ways to increase the clarity of a message.
3. *Explain* the basic differences between a speech and a written work, and *prepare* a speech using an oral style.
4. *Explain* stylistic methods of giving a speech impact.
5. *Discuss* how language, ideas, and people interrelate.
6. *Outline* a program for developing effectiveness in oral style.

John F. Kennedy once stated of Winston Churchill: "He mobilized the English language and sent it into battle." Kennedy's observation reflects an appreciation for the power of language. The proper words and word combinations can bind a people together, create understanding, stimulate concern, and inspire meaningful action. Words can also enhance our thinking through generating, shaping, and refining thoughts.

But language is a double-edged sword that frequently limits and distorts our thinking and spreads confusion, error, and prejudice. To avoid the traps of language and utilize its vast resources one must (1) understand how words, ideas, and people interrelate, and (2) evolve a style of language usage based on such understanding. This chapter should speed your progress toward these goals.

Sharpening the Meaning in Your Mind

As John C. Condon, Jr., states, "Learning to use language intelligently begins by learning how not to be used by language."[1] A group of language scholars known as general semanticists have alerted us to some significant traps of language, ways in which language can distort our thinking.[2] Let us examine some of the most common traps of language and ways to avoid them.

Language Can Freeze Our View of Some Reality

Words are like still pictures of action scenes. Persons, places, and things constantly change whereas the words used to describe them tend to remain constant. As a result, our perceptions of realities often remain constant. For example, we may form the static impression that "Pam is lazy" when, in fact, Pam has *become* an industrious individual.

To avoid the first trap of language: (1) become conscious of the continually changing character of all nature; and (2) mentally or verbally *date* your words and descriptions; for example, Pam (of 1968), World Communism (of 1948), Ford automobiles (of 1977), America (of 1932).

Language Can Blind Us to Differences

A word or phrase can provide a convenient shorthand designation for a large number of persons, places, or things that have

---

[1]John C. Condon, *Semantics and Communication* (New York: Macmillan, 1966).

[2]The pioneer work in general semantics is Alfred Korzybski's *Science and Sanity, an Introduction to Non-Aristotelian Systems and General Semantics* (Lancaster, Pa.: The Science Press Printing Co., 1933). A very readable account of the types of general semantics concepts discussed in this chapter is Irving J. Lee's *Language Habits in Human Affairs: An Introduction to General Semantics* (New York: Harper & Brothers Publishers, 1941).

something in common. We can, for example, use the word *desk* to avoid having to list all the characteristics of a desk. Abstractions can also serve to heal or inspire through helping people transcend their differences. While feelings over the Civil War still simmered, Southerner Henry Grady visualized for his northern audience "the American citizen"—"the sum of Puritan and Cavalier, for in his ardent nature were fused the virtues of both, and in the depths of his soul the faults of both were lost."[3]

Despite the occasional advantages of ambiguity, language often blinds us to important differences in our world. For example, a statement beginning with "The Baptists believe that" ignores the existence of numerous Baptist denominations and of numerous differences between individuals within each of those denominations.

To avoid the second trap of language: (1) become more sensitive to differences; (2) mentally or verbally *index* your generalized words, for example, Caucasian$_1$, Caucasian$_2$, Professor$_1$, Professor$_2$; (3) qualify general statements; for instance, "Black leaders supported Jimmy Carter, *though there were some notable exceptions.*"

Language Can Contribute to a Two-valued Orientation

Closely related to the previous trap is the two-valued orientation, failure to discriminate beyond making "either-or" judgments. During the 1970 congressional elections Spiro Agnew used language that implied a choice between only two alternatives: "The issue [in the November elections] is whether a free people operating under a representative system of government will continue to govern the United States, or whether they will cede that power to some of the people—the irresponsible people, the lawbreakers . . . ."[4] In reality, voters could select from candidates of varying shades of opinion.

To avoid a two-valued orientation: (1) recognize that almost anything people discuss may be divided into a distribution

[3]Joel Chandler Harris, ed., *Life of Henry W. Grady* (New York: Cassell Publishing Company, 1898), p. 86.
[4]The New York *Daily News*, September 12, 1970.

of categories ranging between two extremes; (2) recognize that categories may interrelate and overlap; and (3) use language that reflects the nuances of reality; try to use terms such as *more* and *less.*

Language Can Mask the "Non-allness" of Our Perceptions

Our senses provide insufficient guides to allow us to know everything about any one subject. Similarly, any description of a subject leaves out details; language represents only parts of some reality, as a map represents only parts of some territory. Therefore, beware of statements such as "these are *the* facts" and "she is *never* on time."

To avoid the fourth trap of language: (1) recognize the partiality of your perceptions and descriptions; (2) indicate the incompleteness of your accounts through the use of "and so forth," or through using qualifying words or phrases such as "Here are some examples" or "From my perspective"; (3) become sensitive to *slanting,* which can add to the distortion caused by the incompleteness of our descriptions.

Stimulating the Desired Audience Meaning

Unless the members of your audience can read thought waves, you will have to communicate with them the way ordinary mortals communicate. Since you cannot transfer meaning directly to them, you must use words and signs to evoke in their minds a meaning similar to the one in your mind. For several reasons, that process is not as simple as it sounds.

Words Don't Mean, People Mean

David Berlo defines *meaning* as "internal responses we make to stimuli; and the internal stimulations that these internal responses elicit."[5] A word *means* to a particular person; a word constitutes a stimulus that evokes a certain thought—a certain referent or set of referents—in an individual's mind. This principle has at least two implications for the speaker.

First, you cannot assume that because a word has a referent for you, it also has one for your listeners. As Figure 4.1 illustrates, you may safely use the word *rocket* when communicating with your roommate, but the word has no referent, no meaning, for a Kenyan tribesman who has never seen a rocket or heard the term. We all encounter some words through our own unique experiences. Familiarity with such words sometimes leads us to use them even when speaking to an audience whose realm of experience differs markedly from our own. Thus, a college student might use the term *grade point average* when talking with those outside the academic community, a mechanic might speak of a *universal joint* to those who know little about automobiles, and a psychology major might use terms such as *target behavior* when speaking to a speech class composed of students whose majors range from music to chemistry.

The second implication is that the meaning a word has for you may not be exactly the same as the meaning it has for members of your audience. A term might have a set of referents for you and a similar but not identical set of referents for your listeners. By failing to take this factor into account you might fail to generate the desired meaning, or, worse, generate an undesired meaning in the minds of the audience. In 1967, George Romney decreased his chances for the Republican presidential nomination by proclaiming that President Johnson had "brainwashed" him on the subject of the Vietnam War. For Romney the term *brainwash* apparently evoked unfavorable connotations only about the *brainwasher* (Johnson), but for thousands of Americans the term also conjured up an unfavorable image of the *brainwashee* (Romney). The term had a particular referent for some of Romney's fellow citizens that it did not have for him: it stimulated a thought in their minds that it failed to stimulate in his.

[5]David Berlo, *The Process of Communication* (New York: Holt, Rinehart, and Winston, 1960), p. 184.

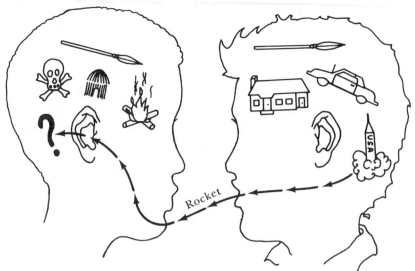

Kenyan tribesman's field of experience and meaningful phenomena. (Does not include rockets.)

Your field of experience and meaningful phenomena. (Does include rockets.)

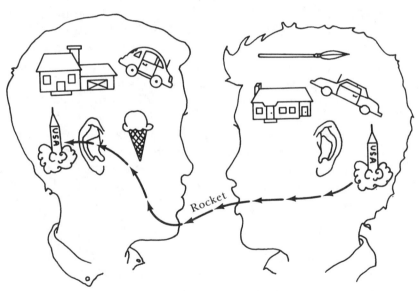

Your roommate's field of experience and meaningful phenomena.

Your field of experience and meaningful phenomena.

Here both share meaning for "rockets," so communication is far easier.

Figure 4.1

The "words don't mean, people mean" principle implies that you should exercise caution in your choice of words and word combinations. The following guidelines should be used in almost any speaking situation, but especially in one in which your audience's realm of experience differs considerably from your own:

1. *Prefer simple to unusual or technical words.* Read the Sermon on the Mount or the Gettysburg Address and notice that one can attain eloquence without using long words. The speaker aspiring to genuine eloquence will consult his or her dictionary and thesaurus often but only to find the right words, not necessarily the long ones. The guiding principle should be to find the shortest and simplest words that say exactly what you mean.

2. *When using an unusual word or using a word in a special sense, clarify your meaning to your audience.* Accuracy and precision, like clarity, characterize an effective style. Occasionally you will have to use an unusual word or use a word in a special sense because you can find no short or simple word that exactly expresses your meaning. In such situations you might ensure audience comprehension of your meaning of the term through one of several methods: (1) restating your idea in different words;[6] (2) giving an example to illustrate what you mean by the term; (3) giving the etymology of the term (breaking it down into its basic elements and tracing its history); (4) defining the term; or (5) explaining how the meaning of the word differs from the meaning of related words.

In a speech delivered in 1961, Martin Luther King, Jr., used several methods to clarify his meaning of the word *love*:

> *Then the Greek language comes out with another word which is called Agape. Agape is more than romantic love, Agape is more than friendship. Agape is understanding, creative redemptive good will to all men. It is an overflowing love which*

---

[6]The next section provides an example of restatement.

seeks nothing in return. Theologians would say that it is love of God operating in the human heart. So that when one rises to love on this level, he loves men not because he likes them, not because their ways appeal to him, but he loves every man because God loves him. And he rises to the level of loving the person who does an evil deed while hating the deed that person does. I think that this is what Jesus meant when he said "love your enemies." I'm happy that he didn't say like your enemies, because it is pretty difficult to like some people. Like is sentimental, and it is pretty difficult to like somebody threatening [sic] your children; it is difficult to like congressmen who spend all of their time trying to defeat civil rights. But Jesus says love them, and love is greater than like. Love is understanding, redemptive, creative, good will for all men."[7]

3. *Prefer concrete to abstract language.* G. Wayne Shamo and John R. Bittner conducted an experimental study which demonstrated that the greater the abstractness of a message (that is, the more referents a message has) the smaller the amount the listener recalls. Shamo and Bittner posit two generalities that help distinguish between an abstract and a concrete message:

"First, individual words have different levels of meaning. Referents that apply to a definite person, time, place, or thing would be more specific than would words with referents which are ideas, concepts, or actions. For example, *art* would be abstract, and a progression of topics with increasingly specific referents would be literature, fiction, novels, Russian novels, *Crime and Punishment,* the latter being the most specific. A second variable directly relating to the abstractness of language would be the structure of the message itself. For example, it would be more abstract to say 'a story' than to say 'the story.'"[8]

[7]Will A. Linkugal, R. R. Allen, and Richard Johannesen, *Contemporary American Speeches: A Source Book of Speech Forms and Principles* (Belmont, Ca.: Wadsworth, 1969), p. 68.

[8]G. Wayne Shamo and John R. Bittner, "Recall as a Function of Language Style," *The Southern Speech Communication Journal* 37 (Winter, 1972): 182–83.

4. *Analyze your audience to ferret out any words which elicit strong emotional reactions.* Remember that a word can have connotative as well as denotative meaning. By carelessly using a word that elicits a strong negative reaction a speaker can erect a barrier which prevents communication. One student, a businessman, recently used the word *planning* when discussing a project with the mayor of a small town. The word stimulated such a strong emotional reaction that further communication became almost impossible. To the mayor "planning" meant the same thing as "zoning," which elicited an image of city government's deciding what would be done with private citizens' land.

A Speech Is Not an Essay with Legs

At least two major differences distinguish a speech and a written work. In terms of intelligibility, perhaps the most important difference relates to the transitory nature of a speech. When you read an essay you can ponder and reflect at will, you can look up the definition of any word you don't recognize, you can reread to determine how a sentence or paragraph relates to the writer's central theme, and you can stop and rest when your mind tires. A speaker's audience doesn't enjoy these luxuries because, as Thomas DeQuincey aptly stated, in a spoken language "each sentence dies as it is born."

Since a spoken language is transitory, an oral style should differ in certain respects from a written style. For example, a speech should contain fewer indefinite pronouns such as *this* and *that,* words that require the listener to recall the noun to which *this* or *that* refers. A second difference is that a speech should contain more restatement than a written work. The following excerpt from a speech on mental health illustrates how restatement can both emphasize and clarify an important point:

> *The fourth observation I want to make is that some patients may have a mental illness and then get well, and then get*

"weller"! I mean they get better than they were before. They get even better than they were before.[9]

The second major difference between a speech and a written work relates to the personal nature of a speech. Whereas the writer sets down thoughts for an unknown audience, divorced both in time and place, the speaker usually faces a specific audience and both speaker and audience react, moment by moment, to the other's personality.[10] The uniqueness of the speaking situation affords the speakers an opportunity, as Kenneth Burke suggests, to become consubstantial with (that is, enter into a "oneness" with) their audience. Language style provides one way to do this.

One way to become consubstantial with an audience is through fulfilling certain of their expectancies by using a style suited to the listeners, the subject, and the occasion. The technical language that an engineer might use in a meeting with his colleagues might grate on the nerves of those assembled for a flower show, and the elevated language of a presidential inaugural address might bore those assembled for a meeting of the Local Hot Rod Association. You should use a style suited to yourself as well as to the subject, audience, and occasion. Unnaturally adopting the language of one's audience can create unintended humor, as some older people recently learned when they used terms such as *groovy* and *far out* when speaking to a teenage audience.

Certain elements should characterize an oral style on almost any occasion. For example, the speaker can identify with her audience through using personal pronouns such as *we*, through asking questions which encourage the audience to think along with her, through using contractions that help establish an informal atmosphere, and through using figurative language to create vivid images that speaker and audience can share. An excerpt from a college oration illustrates the use of all

[9]Linkugel, Allen, and Johannesen, *Contemporary American Speeches*, p. 57.

[10]We normally think of a personality in connection with an individual, but an audience also tends to develop a personality of its own due to the proximity of its members and their sharing of the experience of the speaking situation.

these elements. After quoting an elderly woman's assertion that Americans don't care about American Prisoners of War, Peggy O'Malley stated:

> *"We just don't care": a rather strong accusation whether it comes from the praying lips of six-year-old Ginny [a daughter of a prisoner of war] or that tired old woman. Yet, haven't we done everything possible to secure the release of American prisoners of war—or have we been led down a path of deception by our policical leaders with our rose-colored glasses affixed permanently to our noses by our own indifference.* [11]

Although an oral style tends to increase a speaker's effectiveness,[12] using such a style may not come naturally at first. Because the instruction most students receive in discourse is in the area of writing, they tend to use a written style when preparing speeches. You might find these suggestions useful in combating this tendency:

1. *Develop an extemporaneous attitude.* Speakers who use an extemporaneous delivery, as opposed to a memorized or manuscript delivery, coin their language during the act of speaking. This flexibility usually results in their having a more informal attitude toward the speaking situation and, concomitantly, more informal language. If you think of yourself as engaged in communicative interaction with your hearers and make adjustments based on audience feedback, you will tend to use an oral language. The prac-

[11]Peggy O'Malley, "The Numbered Days: An Oration," *Winning Orations* (Interstate Oratorical Association, 1972), p. 23.

[12]Thomas found that a speech containing many of the elements commonly associated with an oral style—"specific words, colorful words, informality and simplicity of vocabulary, figurative language, personalization, informality of syntax, questions, and direct questions"—"increases the intelligibility of a speech by 10 percent." (Gordon L. Thomas, "Effect of Oral Style on Intelligibility of Speech," *Speech Monographs* [March, 1956], pp. 48 and 52.) Several other studies have been done on this subject. See, for example, James Gibson et al., "A Quantitative Examination of Differences and Similarities in Written and Spoken Messages," *Speech Monographs* (November, 1966), pp. 444–51.

tice of remaining before your audience and answering questions after your speech also helps to develop an extemporaneous attitude and, in turn, an oral style of language.

2. *If you write out any of your speech, you might use as guides a list of distinctions between oral and written discourse.* For example, if you find the words *you are* in your first draft, you might change them to the contraction *you're.* The list below might prove helpful:

   (1) Oral language includes more contractions.
   (2) Oral language includes more personal pronouns.
   (3) Oral language includes more questions.
   (4) Oral language includes more concrete words.
   (5) Oral language includes words with fewer syllables.
   (6) Oral language tends to be more figurative.
   (7) Oral language includes more restatement.
   (8) Oral language includes more repetition.
   (9) The syntax of oral language is more informal.
   (10) Oral language includes more interjections.

3. To test the intelligibility of your style try out your speech orally before a friend or group of friends. They can help you locate potential areas of confusion; for example, areas in which you need to incorporate definition or restatement.

Achieving the Desired Impact

We have all heard speeches which were clear yet which had no more impact than a feather dropped on the floor. The person who speaks because he has to give a speech achieves satisfaction when he utters his last word, his message having barely penetrated the skulls of his hearers. The speaker who speaks because he has a speech to give wishes his message to lodge deeply in the memories of his hearers, there to form the basis for further thought and action. He views rhetoric as the "energizer of knowledge and humanizer of truth" and achieves satisfaction only when his message takes "life" in the form of the reasoned behavior of his audience. Such a speaker gives his message force as well as clarity. Thus he strives for directness, and he gives his speech peaks and plains.

Strive for Directness

"The shortest distance between two points is a straight line" runs a principle of geometry. Your speech will have more impact if you apply this principle to your use of language. You can achieve directness in several ways: through avoiding words with affixes such as *un*intentional; through avoiding the interjection of thoughts between your subject and verb; and through careful selection of verbs. The last method is probably the best one. As J. Jeffery Auer states, "The verb is a motor, propelling the whole sentence. If your ideas are to move, the verb must be worked hard."[13]

Carefully scrutinize every use of the verbs *to be, is, are, am, will be, was,* and *were.* In many cases you can substitute more forceful verbs, as these examples demonstrate:

Weak form:	Is deserving of
Strong form:	Deserves
Weak form:	It is my opinion that
Strong form:	I think
Weak form:	It is vitally important that this matter be brought to our attention
Strong form:	This matter demands our attention

The speaker should welcome the economy of expression that usually accompanies the use of active verbs. At least one study demonstrates that an economical oral style is more effective than an uneconomical one.[14] This does not contradict our earlier assertion that an oral style should contain more restate-

[13]J. Jeffrey Auer, *Brigance's Speech Communication* (New York: Meredith, 1967), p. 113.
[14]J. E. Ragsdale, Jr., "Effects of Selected Aspects of Brevity on Comprehensibility and Persuasiveness" (Doctoral dissertation, University of Illinois, 1964).

ment than a written style. Economy of style means using the number of words necessary to communicate an idea effectively. Thus, restatement becomes uneconomical in only two circumstances: (1) when it serves no useful purpose: for instance, "This line is straight; it isn't crooked;" (2) when the restatement contains more words than necessary. Although both of the statements below contain restatement, the second is more economical.

It is my belief that your plan is unworkable; we won't be able to put it into practice.

I don't think your plan will work; we can't put it into practice.

Give Your Speech Peaks and Plains

While directness should characterize your entire speech, emphasis should characterize only parts of it. Self-evident though this statement is, we've all heard the lazy speaker whose language style indicated that no part of the speech was more important than any other part. Conversely, we've heard the overzealous speaker whose every sentence reeked with weighty implications. Listening to the first speaker reminds one of the bland diet of an ulcer patient; listening to the second is like being fed a steady diet of chocolate fudge.

A speech should have both peaks and plains because (1) some parts of any speech are more important than other parts, and (2) without the plains the audience wouldn't sufficiently appreciate the peaks. Therefore, you will want to emphasize some parts of your speech by presenting them with special emphasis. Even an important idea may have little impact if presented in bland language. In 1884, Justice Oliver Wendell Holmes, Jr., stated: "It is the moment . . . to recall what our country has done for each of us, and to ask ourselves what we can do for our country in return." In 1916, President Warren G. Harding expressed the same sentiments, but the idea struck at the soul of Americans only when emblazed in the language,

"Ask not what your country can do for you—ask what you can do for your country."

Carefully selected language not only serves as a spear that drives a message to the heart of the listener; it also serves as a handhold for the listener's memory. One speaker made a lasting impression on his audience by summarizing his ideas in these terse, parallel phrases: "a purpose to live for," "a self to live with," and "a faith to live by."

How can you use language to enliven an idea? A common method is to use the attention factor of intensity in choosing words and word combinations. One student recently stressed possible dangers of motorcycling when he asserted: "If you aren't careful, you'll find yourself impregnated in a tree." Locate elements in each of these sentence styles that would have robbed that idea of its impact:

> "You will get hurt if you aren't careful."
> "Those who don't exercise caution in motorcycling often get injured."

An examination of the student's actual statement reveals why it drew gasps and caused eyes to widen. Note that the speaker used the word *you* thereby increasing the chances that his listeners would internalize the idea, withheld the crucial part of the sentence until last, and created a striking image with the phrase "find yourself impregnated in a tree."

Novelty of wording provides a second way to increase the impact of an idea. One speaker used this method in emphasizing the number of students who commit suicide each year. She might have said, "This year an alarming number of students will commit suicide." But a slight departure from the normal pattern served to emphasize the idea: "This year an alarming number of students will choose life (slight pause) after death." Another student condemned the movie, *The Exorcist,* by combining two thoughts that ordinarily seem contradictory. Referring to the actions of those watching the movie she said: "People are fainting and vomiting to their hearts' content."

Whether you choose intensity, novelty, or any other method of giving ideas impact, you will need to plan the language of selected segments of your speech.[15] By giving yourself time to reflect, you stand a greater chance of choosing the most potent word combinations. Turn over ideas in your mind not only when you have pencil in hand but also when performing rote tasks, such as walking to class or bathing. Such an idea will strike the perfunctory speaker as silly, but for the person who wants to convey his message with force, the practice of devoting odd moments to his subject should come naturally. For such a person the ripening, the sharpening, and the wording of an idea will merge into a single process.

Developing Effectiveness in Oral Style

We have thus far focused on some specific ways of using language to clarify one's thinking and to maximize the clarity and impact of a speech. In the long run, however, stylistic effectiveness results less from the application of formulae than it does from one's possession of two intangible qualities: (1) a passion to acquire and share knowledge; and (2) an acute sensitivity to the relationships among ideas, language, and people. A brief case study of the preeminent oral stylist in American history, Abraham Lincoln, illustrates how these qualities intertwine.

During his boyhood Lincoln possessed qualities that would lead to stylistic excellence. He eagerly discussed ideas with visitors to the Lincoln farm, and, according to his own account, whenever he found their remarks incomprehensible he

> . . . *would spend no small part of the night walking up and down and trying to make out some of their, to me, dark sayings. I could not sleep, although I tried to, when I got on such a hunt for an idea until I had caught it; and when I thought I had got it, I was not satisfied until I had repeated it*

[15]The philosophy that a speech should have peaks and plains allows the speaker to use an extemporaneous style (coining most of his language during delivery), yet enliven major points with preplanned forceful language.

over and over; until I had put in language plain enough, as I thought, for any boy I knew to comprehend. This was a kind of passion with me and it has stuck by me; for I am never easy now, when I am handling a thought, 'til I have bounded it north and bounded it south, and bounded it east and bounded it west.[16]

The gregarious Lincoln utilized every speaking occasion, from conversations to public speeches, to sharpen his ideas and refine his expression of these ideas. But he also respected the written word, both prose and poetry. He avidly read books and periodicals, and "he learned to appreciate the value of the pen as an instrument to formulate and record his thought, and the more clearly, forcibly, and elegantly to express it."[17]

The giants among oral stylists seem to share the qualities that Lincoln possessed. Their quest for knowledge and their rigorous efforts to improve their style became inseparable and mutually reinforcing processes. The habits of such people reveal some interrelated methods that tend to lead toward excellence in oral style.

Find Knowledge Worth Sharing

Worthwhile ideas and information cannot be separated from effective style any more than the heart can be separated from the body. Attempting to give inane or half-developed ideas impelling expression is as fruitless as applying make-up to a manikin. Ideas were the prime movers of men such as Daniel Webster, Lincoln, and Churchill, people who formulated thoughts that they felt deserved clear and powerful wording. Ideas also provide impetus to the medical doctor who wishes to share vital information about good health habits, the farmer who wishes to tell others of an effective agricultural technique,

[16]Quoted in Mildred Freburg Berry, "Abraham Lincoln: His Development in the Skills of the Platform," *History and Criticism of American Public Address,* II, ed. William Norward Brigance (New York: Russell and Russell, 1960), p. 830.

[17]John G. Nicolay, *The Christian Century,* 25 (1894), p. 825.

the reformer who wishes to correct a social abuse, and the educator who wishes to lead students to a life of discovery.

Our modern world, saturated with books, newspapers, magazines, and television messages, provides us with unprecedented opportunities for learning. However, the bombardment of message stimuli combined with our hurried life style is producing a society of "instant experts," people who glean a smattering of information from a newspaper while gulping a cup of coffee and listen to the "hour's lead story" while dressing for class. Why should we ponder yesterday's happenings when our time is limited and a "news update" awaits us?

The would-be stylist absorbs many of the facts that the mass media provide daily, but he also takes time for the people, literature, plays, and the like, that cause one to pause and consider the values and philosophies that give structure to facts. Like Lincoln, today's thinker ruminates on an idea until he has bound it north, south, east, and west. In the process he uses language to refine his thoughts, and he develops thoughts worth sharing.

Develop an Extensive Speaking Vocabulary

The person with an active desire to acquire knowledge naturally stretches the boundaries of his vocabulary. But the instantaneous nature of speech places special demands on the oral communicator. A writer can take his time while trying to think of the best word for a given concept, and if this fails he can consult a thesaurus. A reader may find slight familiarity with a word sufficient to help her recognize it within a given context, and if this fails she can consult a dictionary. However, a speaking vocabulary embraces the ability to retrieve instantly from one's mind the best word for an idea, audience, and situation, and the ability to pronounce this word correctly.

The speaker, therefore, must hunt words, securely capture them, and make them his permanent possessions. A few commonsense hints can aid in this safari:

1. *Read and listen widely.* New words more often appear in new territory than in familiar habitats. Those who go beyond

their field of specialization or their primary interest to new authors, speakers, and subjects, acquire words appropriate for a wide variety of audiences and speaking situations.

2. *Determine precise meanings and pronunciations.* This requires not only looking up words and pronouncing them aloud but examining synonyms to determine shades of meaning. Moreover, the speaker observes how words affect different people emotionally and how the meanings vary from person to person.

3. *Use more words.* For most people this is a habit that must be cultivated. When writing use *Roget's Thesaurus.* When conversing or giving speeches tax your memory to find the best word for your idea and your audience. With practice an increasing number of words should become instantly retrievable.

Acquaint Yourself with the Resources of Language

Despite the innumerable ways of weaving words together, some people fail to recognize the vast resources of language. To discover the ways of making an audience understand, care, and act, one needs to master English grammar, examine stylistic methods, and observe effective style in action by reading and listening to masterpieces in literature and rhetoric.

Since a speech should evidence a conversational quality, speakers often sprinkle their remarks with sentence fragments and slang. Still, the effective speaker understands the basic structure, the grammar, of language no less than a good mechanic understands the basic structure of a motor. Winston Churchill credited much of his success as a speaker to his boyhood grounding in the King's English. Churchill recalled that his failure to be promoted to Latin proved a blessing: "I gained an immense advantage over the cleverer boys . . . . I got into my bones the essential structure of the British sentence— which is a noble thing." Mastery of grammar—which is becoming a lost art, even among college graduates—requires hard work and sometimes inspires boredom; but it is the foundation of good style.

The second way to discover the resources of language involves studying stylistic methods uncovered by scholars who have investigated language usage. These examples illustrate a few of the sources of language power:

1. The *simile,* signaled by words such as *like* or *as,* can spark a light of understanding by comparing the unknown with the known or the abstract with the concrete. Jesus Christ created a powerful simile to condemn the hypocrisy of an audience: "Alas for you, lawyers and Pharisees, hypocrites! You are like tombs covered with whitewash; they look well from the outside, but inside they are full of dead men's bones and all kinds of filth."[18]

2. The *metaphor,* since it omits words such as *like* or *as,* can increase the emotional impact of a comparison.[19] At Gettysburg Lincoln used a metaphor verbally to wrest life from death. Surrounded by the shallow graves of rotting soldiers he pictured a *living* nation, experiencing a *rebirth* of freedom.[20]

3. The *image* can transport listeners through time and space to some harsh reality or some distant hope. In 1963 Martin Luther King visualized for his massive audience a future for which to strive. The following excerpt is one of five paragraphs which revealed King's image: "I have a dream that one day on the red hills of Georgia, the sons of former slaves and former slave owners will be able to sit down together at the table of brotherhood."

[18]Matthew 22:27 (The New English Version).

[19]An experimental study which has been replicated several times indicates that a speech containing a metaphorical conclusion can be substantially more persuasive than a speech whose conclusion contains no metaphor. (Waite Bowers and Michael Osborn, "Attitudinal Effects of Selective Types of Concluding Metaphors in Persuasive Speeches," *Speech Monographs* [June, 1966], pp. 147–55.)

[20]An analysis of Lincoln's metaphor appears in: Michael Osborn, "Orientations to Rhetorical Style," in *Modules of Speech Communication,* ed. Ronald L. Applbaum and Roderick P. Hart (Chicago: Science Research Associates, 1967), p. 10. Those who wish a more extensive treatment of the resources of language will find Osborn's work most illuminating.

4. The *rhetorical question* can heighten audience involvement in a speech through eliciting at least a silent response from the listeners. John F. Kennedy used these rhetorical questions in his Inaugural Address: "Can we forge against these enemies a grand and global alliance, North and South, East and West, that can assure a more fruitful life for all mankind? Will you join me in this historic effort?"
5. *Repetition* can have a hammer-like effect, driving a point deeper into an audience's mental and emotional being. Winston Churchill used repetition to rally the English people in their war with Germany: "We shall fight on the beaches, we shall fight on the landing grounds, we shall fight in the fields and in the streets, we shall fight in the hills."
6. The *antithesis* can jar an audience's consciousness through the parallel construction of contrasting ideas. Kennedy used this device several times in his Inaugural Address: "Let us never negotiate out of fear. But let us never fear to negotiate."

A study of grammar and of stylistic devices carries one only part of the way toward stylistic excellence. You need also to see and hear good style in action, wedded to the ideas it was invented to express. To discover the riches of language seek good literature written on a variety of subjects in a number of forms and by a wide range of authors. Also listen to speeches delivered on different types of occasions by a variety of speakers to contrasting types of audiences. In the process you should develop an appreciation for good style and a feel for the infinite number of ways in which language can be used.

Cultivate Stylistic Flexibility

Improvement in style as with improvement in any area of life ultimately results from application and practice. A broad-based program of writing and speaking should help develop the stylistic flexibility needed to adapt to a variety of audiences and occasions.

In the tenth book of his *Institutes,* Quintilian states that "It is in writing that eloquence has its roots and foundations; it is writing that provides the holy of holies where the wealth of oratory is stored, and whence it is produced to meet the demands of sudden emergencies." Writing allows us to look at the wording of an expression and repeatedly revise it in thought and language until it defies improvement. The most effectively worded passages normally result from inspiration plus the hard work associated with rigorous rewriting.

The importance of stylistic revision poses a dilemma for the speaker: How can one achieve the potency of expression that comes from refining the wording in advance and still achieve the spontaneity and flexibility that many speaking occasions demand? One solution lies in a diversified speaking program through which a speaker can evolve a stylistic "hybrid vigor." In the animal and plant kingdoms *inbreeding,* the mating of related parents, allows undesirable recessive genes to cause certain weaknesses in the offspring. Conversely, *crossbreeding,* the mating of different varieties of the same species, cancels out the recessive genes thereby resulting in an offspring with hybrid vigor.

Similarly, total concentration in a single type of oral communication (for example, manuscript speaking, extemporaneous speaking) leaves one with stylistic weaknesses, whereas the utilization of a variety of types of oral communication allows one to capitalize on the strengths of each and overcome the weaknesses of each. (See Figure 4.2.) The speaker should de-

	Oratory, Manuscript Speaking, Memorized Speaking	Extemporaneous Speaking, Debate, Conversation
Strengths	Allow speaker to refine carefully thoughts and polish style in advance.	Encourage spontaneity and utilization of feedback.
Weaknesses	Discourage spontaneity and utilization of feedback. Often result in excessive formality.	Often result in a style lacking in economy, variety, and potency.

Figure 4.2

velop a polished style yet one sufficiently flexible to accommodate varied ideas, purposes, audiences, and occasions.

Summary

Since language is a tool for forming and expressing thoughts, we should evolve styles of language that sharpen our thinking and that maximize the clarity and impact of our messages. An effective style enables us to avoid major traps of language: (1) language can freeze our view of some reality; (2) language can blind us to differences; (3) language can contribute to a twovalued orientation; and (4) language can mask the "nonallness" of our perceptions.

Achieving maximum clarity in a speech demands that one adjust to variations in word meanings from person to person and use an oral rather than a written style of language. Achieving maximum impact requires adopting a direct style and giving the speech "peaks and plains."

Suggestions for developing an effective oral style include: (1) find knowledge worth sharing; (2) develop an extensive speaking vocabulary; (3) acquaint yourself with the resources of language; and (4) cultivate stylistic flexibility.

Finally, the effective oral stylist has a healthy respect for ideas, language, and people, and comes to understand the subtle relationships among them.

EXERCISES ❧

1. Keep a one-week log of the traps of language that you find in your own written and oral communication and in that of others.

2. On April 7, 1976, then presidential aspirant Jimmy Carter used the term *ethnic purity*. Using periodicals from your library examine the context of Carter's remarks and comments made by others about his remarks. Identify what you perceive to be the reason for Carter's communication failure, and indicate how he might have avoided the failure. Be prepared to discuss your conclusions in class.

3. Reword each of the following, making each more forceful:
    "Is indicative of" (use only one word)
    "As they were walking across the street" (use only five words)
    "It was last year that I was hit in the eye by a professional boxer." (use five fewer words)

4. Convert one of your old essays to a speech, striving for an oral style, maximum clarity for the classroom audience, and maximum impact on your classroom audience.

5. Assume that you're to speak on the subject of women's rights to a moderate-to-liberal group of women assembled for a faculty wives luncheon. Determine how you would use language in an effort to become consubstantial with your audience. Identify, for example, words you should use and others that you should avoid using.

6. During one of your classroom speeches, set as one of your goals the avoidance of these responses on the part of the members of your classroom audience: (1) I don't understand what you meant by one of the words you used; (2) Your use of one word generated such an emotional reaction that I "tuned out" part of your speech; (3) Your language usage called attention to itself; and (4) Your language usage was so bland it made me sleepy. When orally critiquing other students' speeches, use these criteria to help you pinpoint stylistic problem.

7. Prepare a cross between an extemporaneous and a manuscript speech. Work from an outline, and coin most of your wording while delivering the speech. However, give the speech peaks by including a few memorized, forcibly worded segments.

Delivering the Speech*

❦ **5**

*By Lee Mitchell.

OBJECTIVES ᙍᢌᢒ

After completing this chapter, you should be able to:

1. *Determine* the amount of practice necessary for your speaking assignments.
2. *Arrange* a room to best accommodate your speaking situation.
3. *Understand* the role of nonverbal communication in a public speech.
4. *Use* eye contact more effectively.
5. *Use* your voice to communicate your ideas more efficiently.

Preparation

The more spontaneous a speech seems, the better it usually goes over. An audience has come to hear a speech, not to listen to someone reading material which any one of them might just as easily have read for himself. For this reason the experienced speaker generally avoids reading a speech except for certain quotations or statements where exact wording is more important than spontaneity.

This is not to say, however, that the major points should not be written out rather completely beforehand. In most instances they should be. One reason is to make sure that it is properly organized, that it has a minimum of repetition, that the speaker's thought is going somewhere, and that all the important points are covered in the most effective language.

But after the main points are written, the speaker's preparation has only begun. His next task is to rehearse what he has written, with all main points in the correct order until he can speak it without having to fumble for the right phrasing or think of what comes next. An audience quickly becomes impatient with a speaker who hesitates or seems unsure of himself. The speaker who has prepared properly knows what he is going to say; he seems sure, and he has no need to hesitate.

Speaking from Notes

Even when a speech has been perfectly prepared a speaker needs something to serve as a guide so that no important arguments or examples are overlooked in the heat of the moment and so that facts and figures are accurately given.

Many speakers prefer to put their notes on cards. Ordinarily, each card carries but one note in the form of a short topic sentence, a phrase, or a single word serving as a reminder. (See Chapter 8.)

Those who use cards prefer them over all other forms of notes because they are easy to follow, easy to handle, and can be arranged to take advantage of unexpected shifts in the response of the audience. Also, notes in card form seem to allow a speaker more room to improvise or to expand or condense his material according to the needs of the moment. Cards are firmer and easier to shuffle than pieces of paper, they make less noise in a microphone, and they are less likely to blow away if a breeze comes up. The 4 by 6 inch size fits easily into a side coat pocket from which it can be drawn unobtrusively. Some speakers like to begin with all the cards in one pocket and as the notes are used up, dispose of them by slipping them into the pocket on the opposite side. Others start by spreading out all their cards on the speaking stand like a hand in solitaire, then as the cards are referred to they are turned face down. Printing out the notes on each card in fairly large letters with a felt-tip pen is good; it makes the notes easy to read if the light is poor. It might also make it possible for the speaker to dispense with his glasses.

There are many other systems of notes, such as the "idiot cards" of the television studio, or projections upon some special surface which can be made visible to the speaker but not to his audience, but since none of these is likely to be available to the beginning speaker, they need not be considered here.

Practice

Nothing will ever take the place of thorough practice. The best thought-out presentation is still only an idea, the best and most carefully composed speech only a plan until, by rehearsing it over and over, the speaker has made it completely his own.

It is important that the speech be practiced out loud in the voice which will be used on the platform so that the speaker gets used to the sound of his own voice and his own phrasing. The great Greek orator, Demosthenes, is reported to have rehearsed his speeches on the seashore where he had to raise his voice above the roar of the surf. Any kind of extraneous noise—wind in the trees, the hum of machinery, traffic, children playing—make for better rehearsal than the unnatural silence of some isolated place. No audience is ever completely quiet except at very rare moments of high tension. Most of the time the speaker is accompanied by the rustling of programs, creaking chairs, coughing, whispered comments, and sometimes by applause, booing, or sullen murmurs. A speaker has to get used to speaking loudly enough to be heard above extraneous noises.

Whatever the practice situation, the speech must be rehearsed until the sequence of ideas and the wording of the main points is so firmly fastened in the mind that it cannot be forgotten or disrupted by unexpected reactions of the listeners. At the same time, one must practice expanding and contracting each point so that the ultimate presentation can be adjusted to its particular audience.

It is also necessary to rehearse answers to questions likely to be asked from the floor. And of course no one should attempt to speak in public without rehearsing the measures he will take to deal with interruptions and emergencies of various kinds, such as microphone failure, someone in the audience fainting, or the sudden change in the weather which makes an audience restless.

The best place to practice would be the same room in which the speech is going to be given, for there one could learn to feel at home with the acoustics, the space, and the other physical conditions affecting the speech. This is seldom possible, however. The next best place for practice would be a room resembling the place in which the speech will be given. When no such space is available, then the largest and most open of the available places is always the best. The worst place is the smallest and quietest room. Out-of-doors is always excellent and the presence of extraneous noise helps the speaker to speak up at the same time that it masks the sound of his voice from others and helps him to feel less self-conscious about his rehearsing. However, a man rehearsing a speech in his own back yard is hardly going to attract much attention; certainly nobody is going to arrest him for it.

Practice sessions produce the best results when they are spread out over several days at least, with enough time between (half a day is ideal) for the mind to mull over the subject. Inexperienced speakers often attempt to cram too much practice into too short a time and the result is often stiff and unconvincing, leaving the impression with the audience that the speech has been learned by rote.

Control of Time

One should always practice with a clock in sight so that the speech can be fitted into the time allowed for it. People today, accustomed to the close timing of everything in television, have very little patience with the speaker who runs over his time. Even a person of some renown may have people walk out on his speech when it runs too long (even though they may have nowhere better to go) merely because they are used to closely timed and usually rather brief speeches. Only by rehearsing with his eyes on the clock can the beginning speaker learn to control an audience of listeners habituated to television timing.

Some speakers like to use, instead of a clock, a kitchen timer that can be set to show elapsed time, with a bell which rings when the time is up. In earlier days speakers liked to rehearse in front of an hour glass where they could see the sand running and see also how much was left.

When a speaker has perfected his timing, he knows beforehand just how much time he will need for each point he has to make, especially for his conclusion, so that as he approaches the end of his speech, he has reserved ample time to sum up, underscore main points, and arrive finally at an impressive and unhurried closing. When a speaker has not perfected his timing he usually gives too much time to his opening remarks and thus arrives at the most important part of his speech, the conclusion, with not enough time left. Then in the attempt to get it all in before his time runs out he talks faster, sacrificing control, emphasis, and intelligibility just when he needs them the most.

Place and Audience

A room seating fifty or sixty people fairly close to each other presents no serious problem to the speaker. But when the room is large and the audience scattered around in it, or seated so that a dozen rows of empty chairs separate the speaker from the nearest listener, speaking becomes much more difficult. Speakers confronted with such an audience generally encourage the people to move down to the nearer seats and to sit closer together. Failing this, the speaker may move himself closer to his audience, coming down among them. The more scattered the audience, the harder it is to talk to; if it cannot be persuaded to congregate, the speaker must move himself to where he can make effective contact with his listeners.

From the speaker's point of view the lighting is best when the individual members of the audience can be seen easily enough for the speaker to judge their response. From the point of view of the listener the lighting is adequate when the speaker's face can be seen without effort, that is to say when he is lighted brightly enough from a favorable angle against an agreeable background.

When the audience is dimly lighted it may take several

minutes before the speaker can distinguish individuals and speak to them rather than to the group in general. In the meantime his impulse will be to come down to the edge of the platform in the attempt to get closer to his auditors. This impulse has to be guarded against because it may result in the speaker getting in front of the light so that his face is in the dark. The audience then has such difficulty seeing his expression that it may not be able to pay attention for very long.

Ideally, a speaker should be easy to see, standing out clearly against a background which makes him agreeable to watch for some time, and which contains nothing whatsoever to distract the attention of the observer. Unfortunately, such backgrounds are not very common. Instead, there are sunlit windows, picture-hung walls or blackboards covered with hieroglyphics. There are, however, a number of things that a speaker can do to decrease the competition with his background. If there are windows behind him making his background brighter than his face there are also usually curtains that can be drawn or shades that can be lowered. If there is a blackboard, he can at least erase the material written on it. Many a student's classroom speech has been ruined because he neglected to clean the blackboard behind him and so ended up competing for the attention of the audience with maps or mathematical formulae left behind from some previous class.

If the background is too "busy" with boldly patterned wall paper, for example, or too strong in color, it may be possible for the speaker to stand somewhat further out from it and thus diminish the competition.

Acoustics

When the room in which one is speaking is large enough to hold more than three hundred people the acoustics become important. If the room has a tiled floor, high ceiling, many windows, or brick walls, there is certain to be a good deal of echo. Echoes make hearing more difficult by blurring the sound of the voice. Actually, there is enough sound for hearing but the words are more difficult to understand because they are reflected several times and the different reflections overlap each other. The remedy for this is always the same: speak more slowly, space out the words, and separate the phrases so that the echo has a chance to die down. This will keep the reverberations from one phrase from impinging upon the one following.

Rooms having curved or irregular walls or ceilings often have uneven acoustics. The irregularities tend to focus the sound so that in some spots the voice is easy to hear, while in others where there is a minimum of reflection (called "dead spots") hearing is difficult. The person in the audience who calls "louder" is usually seated in one of these dead spots. If the speaker can persuade him to move, the listener will, as a rule, be able to hear well enough.

When speaking in any large room, it is good practice to spend a half hour or so beforehand familiarizing oneself with the acoustical peculiarities of the place. No two places are ever exactly alike in this respect; it is important to know the special traits of the particular room in which the speech is to be given. One should do this with the help of another person who will move about from place to place while listening to the speech and give some signal to indicate areas of the room which are particularly good or bad for hearing.

The Speaking Stand

The smaller the room in which the speech is given the greater the barrier which a speaking stand seems to create between speaker and audience. In a very large room—one seating three or four hundred or more—it seems natural enough to see a person addressing an audience from behind a speaking stand, especially if he is using a microphone. But when the room is small enough to permit a more informal presentation, the less the stand obtrudes between speaker and audience the better the effect.

The principal purpose of the speaking stand is to hold notes at a convenient height for quick reference. The stand is not a support for the speaker; it is not something to hold, to hide behind, or to lean on. Experienced speakers generally prefer, when possible, not to speak from behind the stand but rather from one side, close enough perhaps to glance now and then at notes but not close enough to appear to depend upon either stand or notes.

The Microphone

With increasing frequency, microphones are encountered in the places where speeches are made. Often they are installed as a fixture of the speaker's stand, regardless of the size of the room or its seating capacity. In most such situations the microphone merely amplifies the voice, compensating in no way for whatever acoustical peculiarities the room may possess. Only in banquet and assembly halls built quite recently are multiple-speaker installations likely to be found.

If the room seats fewer than two or three hundred, one's voice can usually be heard without amplification. If this is the case, it is better to turn off the microphone and speak without it. If, because of the size of the room, the microphone is indispensable, the speech must be rehearsed with the microphone. This is best done with the help of another person who can move about the room, listening from various spots and telling one how loudly to speak and how close to the microphone. Ordinarily the voice need be no louder than in normal conversation. Six or eight inches between the microphone and the mouth of the speaker is usually about right. But sometimes both the volume of the voice and the distance from mouth to microphone will have to be adjusted to overcome oddities in the acoustics of a particular room.

Platform Presence

A group of people gathered together in one place does not constitute an audience. Not until its attention has been focused upon a common center of interest does it become one. It will continue to be an audience only as long as it continues to listen as a group. When any significant number of the group stop listening the audience disintegrates and becomes again a mere collection of individuals. The first purpose of the speaker, therefore, must be to concentrate the attention of his hearers and to keep them listening. Without such centered and held attention he has no audience at all.

It is helpful to remember that the people who form the group are there for a reason: they want to enjoy the speech; they want to be interested, informed, or thrilled, and they hope for the best. They do not expect to be bored. Because of this the speaker who initially communicates his own interest and enthusiasm, whatever his subject or point of view, is much more likely to arouse their interest and to succeed with his speech.

In actuality, the speech begins as soon as the speaker gets up and starts toward the platform, for this is when the people who are there prepare to listen and thus begin to become an audience. Good humor, self-assurance, and eagerness to communicate all show in the manner in which the speaker approaches the platform and makes it his own. Generally, the approach is best when it is lively but unhurried. After taking position it is well to wait a few seconds before beginning to speak. This allows time to take a deep breath, collect one's thoughts, and look over the audience. At the same time the brief delay gives the listeners time to settle down, focus their attention, and get ready to respond to the speech.

The first few sentences should always be genial and usually extemporaneous, with some reference to the specific occasion, the audience, or the place. Then comes the speech that has been prepared.

When the speech is finished one should not be in too great a hurry to leave the platform. A very brief pause following the final words allows the conclusion to sink in. The manner in which the speaker leaves the platform should be appropriate to the particular character of the speech which has just been given. If the speech was a serious one, the manner of leaving the platform should be sober and dignified; if the speech was humorous, the manner of leaving should not be grave, but lighter and more cheerful. Not until the speaker has returned to his place and taken his seat can the speech be said to be truly completed.

Nonverbal Communication

Beginning speakers usually feel awkward and they show it by the way they stand and what they do with their hands. The various ways in which people habitually stand during everyday conversation often look very strange on the platform: hands clasped behind or in front, hands in pockets, arms folded, or feet widely spread. Some apt names have been coined to identify these beginning speakers' attitudes: the "colussus of Rhodes" stance; the "Napoleon"; the "Lincoln lapel grabber"; "the forward fig-leaf," and so forth, until it must seem as if there is no possible posture which has not been tagged with ridicule. Actually, all of these attitudes have been used at one time or another by successful speakers, but always in such a way that the attention was on the speaker and what he was saying rather than the way he was standing or holding his hands.

If the manner in which a speaker stands seems odd to his critic, then he must experiment with other ways until he finds some that suit. If his hands attract attention away from his speaking he might experiment with holding something unobtrusive such as a pencil, note card, or small notebook. Needless to say, none of these should be white or bright in color.

Gestures are easy enough when it is a matter merely of pointing out something or indicating direction or height. The indication of space or volume is more difficult and requires more practice. The most difficult gestures are those which express feelings, such as hopelessness or indifference. For the beginner the best plan is usually to limit the expression of feeling to his voice and manner of speaking, keeping his hands and body quiet or at most, using them to give no more than the faintest hint of feeling.

Eye Contact

The most accomplished speaker is the one who woos his listeners, winning their sympathy, and capitalizing on each indication of their growing interest until in the end they willingly share his point of view. To do this he must first see them; he must get into the habit of looking steadily at them and seeing them clearly as individuals. He must learn to study the response of his listeners in order to judge the effect of his remarks.

This is surprisingly difficult at first. The beginner is likely to be more conscious of himself and his task than of the audience he is trying to win. At first, with the lights in his eyes, all he sees is the dark auditorium and a blur of dim faces. After a few minutes, however, it becomes easier for the speaker to distinguish individuals. Thus, as he becomes able to see his audience better, he gradually enlarges his circle of interested listeners.

It is very important for the individual audience member to feel that the speaker is talking directly to him. Whenever the speaker is close enough to his audience to look directly into the eyes of his listeners, he should do so, for this causes them to accept everything he says as more personal and significant.

From the speaker's point of view, the only members of the audience worth speaking to are those who appear to be interested; their interest gives one a considerable "lift," and makes the speech easier. Other individuals who at first appear to be bored, skeptical, or hostile, are best ignored until they begin to show interest. The effort of winning them over often takes too long and tends to make the speech too tense and strained for comfortable listening. If one worries about winning the indifferent listeners while he is speaking, it is certain to spoil the tone of the speech.

Eyeglasses are a severe hindrance to eye contact because of the way they reflect the light and make the eyes of the speaker hard for the audience to see. For this reason it is best, if possible, to speak without one's glasses. Of course, the individual members of the audience may become indistinguishable, but this is sometimes a help since one can then assume that they are all paying rapt attention. As for them, as long as the speaker is looking in their direction he will seem to be looking right at them; they have no way of knowing what he actually sees. How many political candidates do you see wearing glasses on the platform? Very few. This is why.

Mannerisms

Practically everyone we know has his or her own collection of personal mannerisms and random actions. One person pulls his ear when he is deep in thought, another one always straightens his tie before he enters a room, a third scratches her head whenever she is puzzled. Interesting as such mannerisms are, none of them is much help to a speaker in public; all of them distract attention and take away from the effectiveness of the speech as a whole. The initial problem lies merely in the fact that the speaker is unaware that he is shuffling his feet, playing with his watch, rubbing his nose, or vocalizing his pauses, and does not realize that these distractions are annoying and distracting.

A speaker needs a critic who will point out to him the particular bad habits which mar his delivery. Once he knows what they are, he can, by determined practice, rid himself of them.

The Vocalized Pause

Of the mannerisms, one of the most common and certainly the most irritating to listeners is the vocalized pause. This is the familiar "and-uh" habit that so many people have, the hemming and hawing that fills in the spaces between the successive thoughts. A speaker addicted to vocalized pause will, for example, say: "his next task is to memorize what he has -uh-written, while the man who has prepared always knows what he is going to -uh-say; he then has no need to -uh-hesitate." This is a vicious habit. And it is nothing but a habit. Yet, many otherwise good speakers fall into it simply through carelessness and inadequate preparation or criticism. In most cases the audience already knows what the next word will be so that their being made repeatedly to wait to hear it annoys them and makes them impatient and restless. The remedy for the vocalized pause is simple. It is merely to stop voicing that "uh" between words and to close up the gap.

Distractions

The items capable of distracting the attention of an audience are practically unlimited in number: latecomers, backstage noises, low flying planes, police sirens in the distance, sputtering or screeching microphones, rattling air conditioners, flickering lights, rustling programs, squeaky chairs, the sudden sound of wind or rain, thunder, babies crying, people leaving early, and so on.

Sometimes, when the distraction is a familiar one, it is possible to ignore it, or simply to raise one's voice and speak right over it. Sometimes it is necessary to pause, saying, "I will resume in a moment," and wait it out. But if the distraction is too loud to be overspoken and goes on too long, the audience will lose its centricity and disintegrate into the same unpolarized group which it was before the speaking began. When this happens there is usually nothing left but to abandon the attempt to deliver the speech. The most important thing in any case is for the speaker to retain his composure and his good humor; not to allow the distraction to irritate him, causing him to display the worst side of his nature to the audience.

The best way to learn how to manage distractions is to practice continually with simulated ones. This requires, during the rehearsal period, an imaginative helper who can attempt to throw the speaker off his balance by introducing unexpected distractions at critical points in the speech. For when the time comes to deliver the speech to the real audience the one thing one can be sure of is that any distractions which occur will certainly come from the least expected source and always at the worst possible point in the speech.

Use of the Voice

Toward the end of the 1976 presidential campaign President Ford grew hoarse and lost his voice. Most people thought it was because he was speaking so often that he wore his voice out. Those acquainted with the art of public speaking knew better: it was not that he was speaking too much but that toward the end of the campaign he was trying too hard and because of this he was straining his voice. In his determination to get his message across he was misusing his voice and in the end it failed him.

If this can happen to a speaker as experienced as President Ford it can happen to anyone. Anyone, that is, who misuses his voice.

When properly used, the voice enables a speaker to make contact and to make sense; first, to reach and hold his listeners and second, to make sure that they understand him.

Making Contact

Reaching an audience means more than merely speaking loudly enough for all to hear. It means practicing (preferably in the hall where the speech is to be given) with a helpful critic-friend to tell how much force is going to be needed. It means practicing to be able to speak to those farthest away without seeming to shout. It means watching those farthest away to see if they are able to listen without effort. It means practicing relaxation in breathing and placing the voice so as to use all of it and not only part of it.

Unpracticed persons when they try to speak louder often raise the pitch of their voices also. This not only makes the voice unpleasantly shrill but also strains the vocal cords. Straining the vocal cords causes hoarseness and ultimately complete loss of voice. Each individual has an "optimum pitch," the level at which his voice is most relaxed, most flexible, and most agreeable to the listener. Every speaker has to find out what his own optimum pitch is and practice until he uses it unconsciously.

Having a well-placed voice, however, is not enough if a speech is going to be more than two or three minutes long, for in order to hold the attention of an audience a speaker must have enough variety in his voice to keep them awake. A flat droning voice or a habit of sing-song inflection will put an audience to sleep every time. Most Americans require considerable practice in order to develop enough variety to keep an audience awake beyond the first five or ten minutes. English, Irish, and Welsh speakers are much more fortunate in this respect because melodic variety is native to their everyday speech.

The manner in which a speaker uses melody and pitch variation, especially in voicing his vowel sounds, determines his success in making his listeners feel as he wants them to feel, whether serious, jovial, sarcastic, or fearful. You can test this by taking some simple statement such as, "I would not have come if you had not called me," and saying it several times with different inflections. It can be made to sound sarcastic, or reproachful, or flippant. You will immediately discover the secret: the way the vowel sounds are managed makes the difference. A statement such as "Meek little Alice played the part of the Lion," can be made to sound amusing and absurd merely by attenuating the "ee" in "meek" and the "i" in "Lion."

Making Sense

Making sense of a speech is a different kind of achievement; it means speaking so that listeners can not only hear but understand. When an audience is large enough, more than a dozen or fifteen people, it means using your voice in a manner somewhat different from that which would be used in ordinary conversation.

With a large audience a speaker must speak much more deliberately than in conversation, with more frequent pauses and more definite punctuation. With an audience of several hundred he cannot speak nearly as fast as he would if he had only two or three listeners. At the same time he must speak much more clearly, carefully pronouncing consonants such as "t," "d," "m," and "p," which are generally slurred in conversation. There is an old saying that "Vowel sounds convey feeling; consonants convey meaning," and it is a good axiom to remember when rehearsing a speech. Unfortunately, the solitary critic-friend is less helpful here because in the absence of an audience speech tends toward conversation.

Speech Defects

No one who hopes to succeed with any audience larger than the circle of his immediate family and friends can afford to have any kind of speech defect. Most of us have defects of some sort or other and in the everyday course of our lives such common defects as lisping, nasality, harsh gutterals, or unarticulated consonants may be acceptable to those who know us. But when a person speaks to a group of any size, especially of strangers, speech defects become painfully apparent. The larger the audience is, the more conspicuous a defect becomes. Speech defects not only distract listeners and mar the impression the speaker is trying to make, they actually make it difficult for an audience to understand what he is trying to say.

Most speech defects are nothing more than bad habits, the results of carelessness in the use of the vocal mechanism. Most can be overcome with determined practice and a little outside help. Nine out of ten times there is no excuse for a speaker to have any defects at all. In any case, one thing is absolutely certain: he will never become a speaker of any consequence as long as his speech is defective.

Summary

Effective speech delivery begins with early preparation. Writing down the ideas to be delivered is the first step, since the process of writing fixes the ideas firmly in the speaker's mind in a well-organized form. This inevitably leads to greater fluency when the speech is presented to the audience. Practice is the second step. Using the written outline of ideas, *stand* in a room at least as large as the room in which the audience will gather, and speak the ideas *aloud* to your imaginary listeners. As you go over the ideas several times, you will find you need the written outline less and will gradually "make the speech your own." You may develop several speaker's notes (on index cards) listing statistical information, direct quotations, and other ideas which you want to be certain to include, and you will find it helpful to use a watch to rehearse carefully the timing of your speech.

Effective delivery also means the speaker must control his audience and the total situation surrounding the speech. This means assuring that audience members are seated compactly, and carefully checking beforehand on items such as acoustics, the speaking stand, the background, and the microphone.

From the moment a speaker rises and approaches the platform he is "delivering" his speech. Once the audience has focused on the speaker everything he says and does, until he is again secure in his seat, communicates something. Eye contact, gestures, stance, vocal qualities—all must blend into a communicative whole. Distracting mannerisms, vocalized pauses, and poor handling of distracting noises or sights can easily ruin a speech and must gradually be eliminated through the use of speech critics and constant practice. Thorough practice, especially with a critic-friend, can also help you determine your optimum pitch, develop vocal variety, discover the proper rate and pause time for the size of the room and audience, and eliminate any slight speech defects you might have.

EXERCISES ❦

1. Observe a speaker outside of your speech class. Write a description of the physical surroundings such as size and type of room. Discuss the speaker's management of eye contact, voice, and bodily activity.

2. Before giving your next speech in class, arrange to have it recorded on audio tape. Have a friend listen with you and evaluate your voice control during the speech.

3. Prepare a short speech in which you demonstrate to the class how to do some activity. The focus of this exercise should be upon using the body as an aid to your speaking.

4. Describe the mannerisms of a speaker who appeals to you. Would these same mannerisms be effective if used by other speakers?

5. Interview someone who does a great deal of public speaking. Find out how this speaker prepares for a speaking engagement. Seek any advice this person can give about improving your speeches.

Using Visual Aids*

6

*By Paul R. Corts.

OBJECTIVES ✌

After completing this chapter, you should be able to:

1. *Appreciate* the use of visual aids in a speaking situation.
2. *Identify* the basic types of visual aids which may be used in a speaking situation.
3. *Select* visual aids appropriate for the particular speech situation.
4. *Identify* basic media forms which may be used in preparing visual aids for speech situations.
5. *Create* appropriate visual aids based upon a knowledge of the rules of preparation.
6. *Use* appropriate visual aids in a speaking situation based upon a knowledge of the rules for use of visual aids.

You are probably familiar with the old saying that a thousand words cannot a picture make. Or put another way, one picture is worth a thousand words. This familiar saying is especially appropriate when considering the use of visual aids in relation to speech-making.

Just as we can say that one picture is worth a thousand words, we can also say that a thousand words amplifying a picture can make that picture worth still more. In other words, visual aids should never overshadow the speaker or the speech, but should rather serve to assist the communication process with the dissemination of information through another sense, the visual. A careful blending of the visual with the oral actually complements both and represents an extremely high order of effective and efficient communication.

One of the most valuable uses of the visual aid is its ability to specify material. A visual presentation is consistently more accurate and reliable than an oral description. This is especially true when dealing with large numbers or large amounts of information and it is often true in making comparative analyses. A visual aid can deal with many numbers by putting them semipermanently in front of the audience visually. This is often more effective than a speaker orally communicating those numbers which are either easily forgotten by an audience or readily run together. Neither of these unfortunate circumstances occurs when large amounts of information are placed in the nature of well-chosen visual aids.

Modern rhetorical theorists, who stress the need for communication and the avoidance as much as possible of even the chances for miscommunication, stress the value of *precise* communication which is made possible through the use of visualization. The process of defining terms, of making certain that those spoken to are receiving a communication as intended by the one speaking, is enhanced by the assistance which a visual aid can give to the oral presentation. Modern communication which is so heavily laden with information dissemination either exclusively, or as a part of a persuasion process, has special needs for the visualization process.

The use of the visual sense in no way detracts from the speaker when visual aids are properly used. In fact, the supporting visual material can free the speaker from the sheer drudgery of merely communicating precise data. The visual aid can actually disseminate the crucial information. This chapter describes basic visual aid types and some general rules to follow in using these materials.

Types of Visual Aids

Chart

The typical chart is used to describe relationships existing among various entities. The most frequently used chart is probably an organizational chart which shows the nature of the relationship between the various parts. In the example provided (Figure 6.1) you see an organizational chart with lines demonstrating different types of relationships which exist. This type of chart is frequently used in business and professional speaking. This is often called a "line-staff" chart.

Graph

Graphs are generally used to aid in disseminating large amounts of information. A graph is also a helpful device to use when making comparisons between or among sets of data.

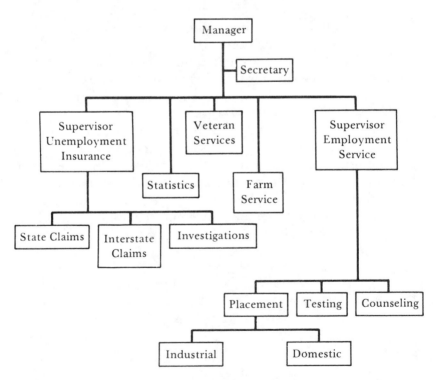

ADMINISTRATIVE ORGANIZATION OF
DEPARTMENT OF ECONOMIC SECURITY

Figure 6.1 *Chart*

Different types of graphs range from a very simple line graph to a more complex picture graph. In the accompanying examples you will find illustrations of a line graph, a pie graph, and a picture graph (Figures 6.2, 6.3, and 6.4). The line and pie graphs are relatively easy to draw. The most complex of the graphs, the picture graph, can be easily and professionally done with the use of commercial materials which are available in most college bookstores. When using a graph to make a comparison, be certain that the graph is highlighted properly to emphasize your intended comparison.

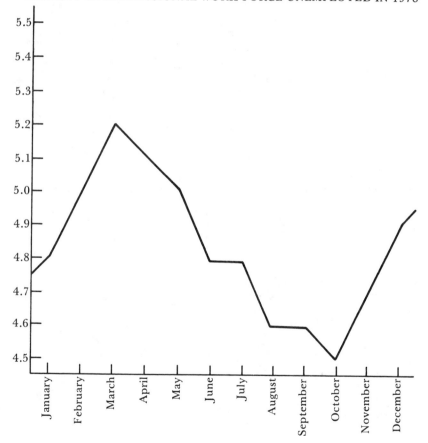

PERCENT OF PROFESSIONAL WORK FORCE UNEMPLOYED IN 1978

Figure 6.2 *Line Graph*

GENERAL FUND BUDGET DOLLAR

Where It Comes From

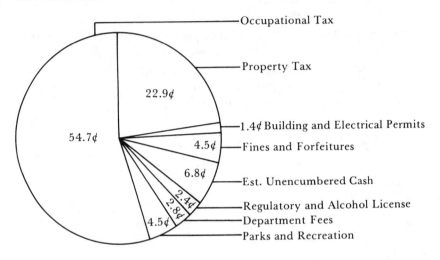

Where It Goes

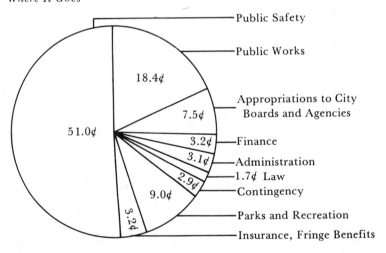

Figure 6.3 *Pie Graph*

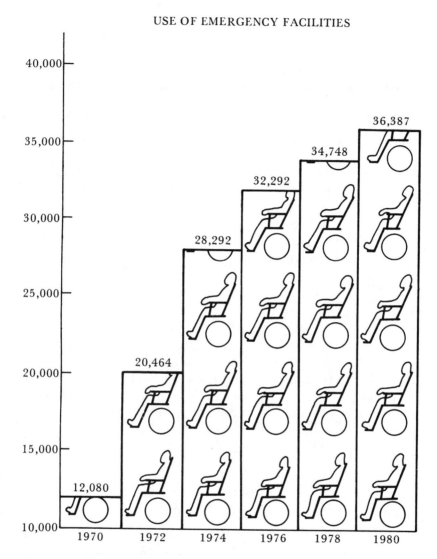

USE OF EMERGENCY FACILITIES

Figure 6.4 *Picture Graph*

Diagram

Diagrams can range from a very simple explanation to an extremely complex series of interrelationships. The basic purpose of a diagram is to demonstrate through the visual sense as clearly as possible the interrelationships of various parts to a whole (Figure 6.5). A very effective diagram can be created through the use of plastic transparency material which can be laid one on top of another. This process is referred to as a transparency overlay and allows a speaker to demonstrate interrelationships of parts to the whole by starting with a very simple diagram on one plastic transparency and then, without removing the first simple diagram, laying another transparency immediately on top of the first. The second transparency will give additional dimensions. This process can be repeated with three, four, or even more transparencies laid one on top of another. Through each step a complex interrelationship is built which allows the viewer to see, step-by-step, the explanation which you are making orally.

Maps

A map is considered a special type of visual aid because of the various functions which a map visually serves. Maps may be used simply to indicate geographical boundaries. However, a map can become very complex when other dimensions are added to simple boundary demarcations. Figures 6.6 and 6.7 provide examples of a simple map and a more complex dimensional map.

Object

Sometimes it is convenient for you to use a real object. To incorporate the use of a real object as a part of your speech, if the object is too large itself, you may use a model which is prepared on a scale to the original. Often an object used as a part of a demonstration has the capacity to be taken apart and put back together so that procedures can be explained in the speech and demonstrated visually with the use of the real object. For instance, if a speaker were making a presentation on the structural aspect of automobile safety, he could use a small model automobile as a real object to demonstrate numerous

WALL SUPPORT FOR BRICK VENEER HOME

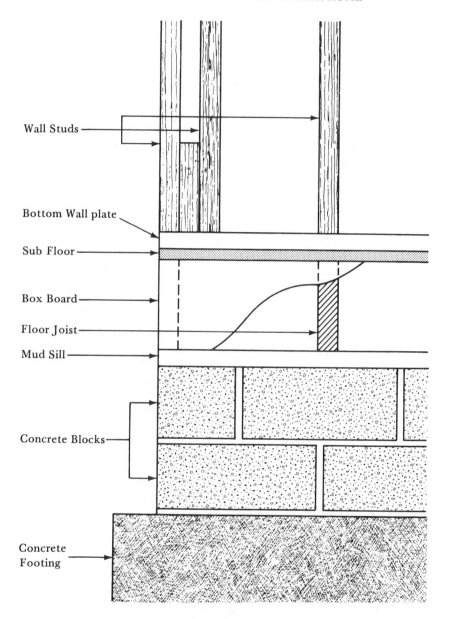

Figure 6.5 *Diagram*

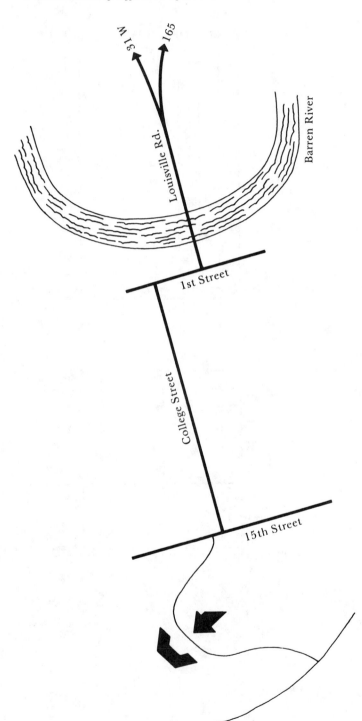

Figure 6.6   *Simple Map*

THE SCIENCE OF WEATHER FORECASTING

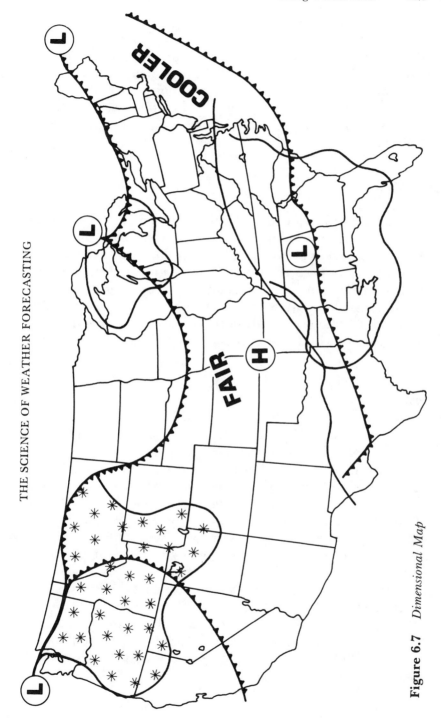

Figure 6.7 *Dimensional Map*

points in the oral presentation. A demonstration can also use a model or real object which may not be taken apart and put back together, but which may simply expose items on the inside which are not normally seen. This type object used in a demonstration is referred to as a "cutaway." In either case, this can be a very useful and practical visual assist to a speech of demonstration.

Cartoon

The success of humor in presenting a speech has always been recognized as an especially good gift. A cartoon can assist a speaker with a visual exaggeration that will create humor. This device can be very successful in disseminating information or in persuading. Not everyone is capable of preparing a cartoon to use as a visual aid in his or her speech, but for those with an artistic touch the use of cartoons can make a fine contribution to an otherwise dull oral presentation (Figure 6.8).

Print

Many students would not recognize that a simple visual aid with nothing more than letter print has the potential for being a very successful visualization. However, lettering and printing words on a posterboard for the sake of saying, "I have a visual aid," will not automatically make a successful presentation. The use of creative lettering coordinated with the oral presentation of a speech can make a success. Type styles, letter size, the dimensions of letters, spacing, and the use of stencils are all important items to consider when a student is preparing a print visual aid. Professional lettering is available in most college book stores in a variety of type styles which allow lettering to be made by rubbing over a carbon letter with a pencil, causing the letter to stick on a posterboard at the desired location. Through the use of this professional adhesive lettering, a student can make a very attractive print visual aid.

A Good Speaker Is........
- on time
- prepared
- organized
- well-groomed
- pleasant

Figure 6.8 *Cartoon*

Photo, Slide, Filmstrip, or Film

Prepared photos, slides, filmstrips, or films are sometimes available and can be used as effective visual aids. Snapshot photos would rarely be appropriate for a speaking situation because of their small size. An 8 x 10 photo might be appropriate for a very small audience if the picture did not have too much detail. Small photos could be transferred to a slide for projection or the speaker could use an opaque projector. However, because of the possible problems involved, beginning speakers should not attempt to use regular photos if any alternative is available. Already prepared slides, filmstrips, or film can be projected to the appropriate size, but the speaker should be aware that film-related visual aids sometimes overpower the speaker. Usually a small amount of film, filmstrip, or slide is sufficient. The beginning speaker should be on guard to keep the audience's primary attention focused on the speaker and the speech, not on the visual aid.

Any type of film, whether a motion picture, a filmstrip, or a slide, is a picture; but a picture can also be shown if it is in print form. As you research for your speeches and find pictures in magazines or books which you believe would be useful visual aids to accompany your oral presentation, keep in mind that most pictures can be reproduced and enlarged in the classroom through the use of an overhead opaque projector.

The most important consideration in using the visuals discussed here is to be aware of their potential for overpowering the speaker. The speaker must carefully plan his visuals so that they will supplement his own performance and add to the total communication act.

Media Forms

Posterboard and Felt-Tip Pen

The typical beginning student faced with a speech assignment calling for a visual aid will select the type of visual aid (chart, graph, diagram, and so on) and then purchase a posterboard and felt-tip pen from the college book store. Ready with these materials, the student will proceed to prepare a "typical" visual aid. This may be the best media form for you to use, but consider the other forms listed below. The value of the posterboard and felt-tip pen is the easy availability of the materials and the relative ease of preparation. If you use this form, be sure to use a large posterboard and make your lettering or drawing large enough to be easily seen by the entire audience. This media form is also especially useful because of its adaptability for almost any visual aid type. Even photos can be mounted on posterboard with print elaboration.

Transparency—Overhead Projector

A transparency is a sheet of clear acetate, normally 8½ × 11 in size, which is used with an overhead projector to project an image onto a screen or wall. Lettering or drawing can be done directly onto the clear acetate sheet with a felt-tip pen. Through special equipment, a transparency can photographically reproduce material from a printed page or a hand-prepared document. The transparency and overhead projector can also team up for an effective on-the-spot presentation which can be used in place of a chalkboard. The transparency has several advantages. First, a speaker can write on the transparency while continuing to face the audience. Second, colors can be used on the transparency which will enliven the presentation. Third, the speaker can move quickly and easily from one acetate sheet to another without erasing the board or boggling with a large and sometimes cumbersome posterboard. Fourth, the transparency provides the option for using an overlay technique which permits the speaker to have a multidimensional presentation by placing one acetate sheet over another to provide step-by-step completion of a visual aid.

Photo, Slide, Filmstrip, or Film

A student speaker will rarely have access to the professional materials required to develop visual aids involving still photo camera shots, slides, filmstrips, or movie film. However, you should be aware of these media types for future possibilities. These film-related visual aids taken specifically for a speech usually require careful planning and setting development which simply is impossible for the student speaker. This media preparation form should not be confused with already produced and available photos, slides, filmstrips, or films which constitute a visual aid type. Photos, slides, filmstrips, or films are visual aid media forms and can be used to display other visual aid types. A chart, graph, or diagram, for instance, could be prepared in slide form for presentation or it could be prepared on a posterboard or transparency.

Opaque Projection

Through the use of an opaque projector, most visual aid types can be projected onto a screen or wall. The opaque projector will project an image from a printed page, a photo, picture, chart or any reasonably flat, unidimensional object. It usually requires no preparation by the speaker since it simply projects an already produced image. Because of the noise associated with this projector, a beginning speaker should carefully plan use of the equipment so that use of this aid does not detract from the speaker. An opaque projector, in contrast to the overhead projector, requires a darkened room which can also be distracting to the audience.

Audio

Although this chapter is entitled "Using Visual Aids," audio aids are usually considered in conjunction with the visual. Student speeches seldom use audio aids but it is a media form you should be familiar with. Cassette audio tapes and small cassette players make this audio aid easily accessible. The change of pace for the audience in hearing another voice can also help hold attention and increase audience interest. A brief oral excerpt from a personal interview is an example of how an audio aid could be used in a speech. If you use an audio aid, be certain the tone quality is clear and that the volume is appropriate for the speech setting.

Rules for Preparation and Presentation

Choose Material Carefully

If you are creating a visual aid which must be placed on some type of object, first decide if you will use posterboard, plastic transparency, film, or some other type material. In dealing with an object for a model for demonstration, carefully choose the particular type object or the appropriate type of model. Regular bond paper is never an acceptable material to use for a visual aid for an audience the size of a typical class. Bond paper is usually too small in size, too flimsy to stand up, and too thin to be opaque. Even in using posterboard, you should be cautioned about its tendency to bend, and its lack of solidity. Many students make excellent plans for using visual aids to accompany speeches only to find that the posterboard visual aid will not stand where it is placed and there is no equipment available to assist in holding the flimsy cardboard. Similarly, if a student plans to use film or a transparency which requires projection, the student should be aware that projectors are extremely noisy and that projection light bulbs frequently burn out, even in the middle of the speech. A student who prepares a very fine visual aid for projection, but who is unable to be heard because the projector makes more noise than the speaker, will not present a successful speech. However, these are really simple problems that can be easily accommodated if the student plans in advance, is aware that these problems may arise, and has a prepared plan for coping with these problems if they develop.

Check the Size

A visual aid, to be successful, must surely be large enough to be easily seen from any part of the audience. A visual aid with small fine detailed print, which forces members of the audience to strain in an effort to see it, will not aid the speaker, but will instead detract from the overall success of the speech. If possible, check visual aids for size in the actual situation in which the visual aids will be used. It is easy to be mistaken on size if you rely solely on your imaginative judgment.

Rehearse With the Equipment

If the visual material requires some type of special equipment, take all precautions to make certain that the equipment can be available for the particular class session. Become familiar with the operation of the equipment so that a smooth transition can be made in the speech. If there are particular problems associated with the use of the equipment, such as noisy or clumsy operation, you should determine through advance preparations and trial runs the effective ways of coping with these problems. If you are inexperienced at using the equipment, don't trust your imagination but actually rehearse with the equipment.

Be Clear

Many visual aids fail to be effective and successful because the audience cannot understand the visual aid. In preparing visual material you will do well to remember that a small amount of information presented within a large framework represents the most successful approach. Considerable open space on a visual aid is important so that a listener can easily and quickly grasp a very specific but limited amount of information from the visual aid. The purpose is defeated if the audience is forced to study considerable minutia. A simple visual aid will be more effective than an overly complex visual presentation.

Be Creative

Not everyone is an artist, but everyone has the potential for presenting a respectable, legible, neat, and colorful visual aid. In preparing visual materials, it is important to remember some of the crucial elements affecting the visual such as color, shape, size, and dimension. These elements, appropriately selected in composing a visual aid, can help the non-artist produce a highly artistic presentation.

Keep Talking

In using a visual aid a speaker should make every effort to continue speaking to the audience while using the visual aid—

rather than turning and speaking to the visual aid itself. Of course, it is a standard rule that the speaker should never turn his back to the audience. This is especially important when projection of the voice is crucial in a large room. Generally, the visual aid should be completed before the speech so that the speaker can devote attention to speaking rather than working on completion of the visual aid. A period of silence in the speech will distract audience attention from the speaker and allow the visual aid to usurp the speaker's central role.

Don't Let the Aid Become the Speech

It is easy for an inexperienced speaker to rely too much on a visual aid to support a speech. The temptation to let the visual aid be the most important factor in the speech is especially overpowering for an inexperienced speaker who finds it more comfortable to let visual material, prepared in advance, replace the speaker as the communicator. A successful visual aid simply must not become the speech.

To avoid this problem, keep the visual aid itself relatively simple and keep your presentation of the aid straight to the point. As you first show the visual aid, orally introduce it with a comment such as "In this graph we can see that . . ."; or "This map locates . . ."; or "This mock-up shows . . . ." Then, while continuing to face the audience as directly as possible, briefly describe orally the essential elements of the visual aid stressing the major point to be seen in the aid. Having completed the use of the visual aid for its intended purpose, quickly and gracefully remove it from sight of the audience so that it will not be a competing stimulus as you continue your speech. As you are physically removing the visual aid, continue the oral presentation of your planned speech.

The amount of time devoted to a visual aid should be related to the total speech. For instance, if you are giving a ten-minute speech and using three visual aids, each aid should normally consume no more than thirty seconds, approximately one-twentieth of the total speech. Excluding a normal introduction and conclusion of a ten-minute speech, three such visual aids would represent approximately one-sixth of the speech.

For the types of speeches presented in a beginning speech course, if visual aids consume more than one-sixth of the speech, they can overpower the speaker and the speech so that the visual aids become the speech.

Summary

Visual aids can be useful additions to effective speech-making. While they should never overshadow or replace the speech itself, visual presentations provide informative, interesting, and supportive material for the speech. Basic visual aid types include charts, graphs, diagrams, maps, objects, cartoons, print, photos, slides, filmstrips, or films.

Media forms used to present visual aids include poster-board and felt-tip pen, transparency for overhead projector, and some type of film, opaque projection, and audio.

In preparing and presenting visual aids, the speaker should choose material carefully, rehearse with the aid, check the size of the aid, and be clear and creative in its presentation. The speaker should always continue speaking while presenting the aid. It is also very important that the visual aid not become the speech.

Although these rules should appear easy to follow, the beginning speaker will find that the biggest problem connected with using visual aids is the difficulty of doing two things at once: speaking while handling an aid. Careful advance preparation, full familiarity with the aid, and rehearsing with the aid can help you use visual aids successfully to make your speech more fully communicative.

EXERCISES ❧

1. Select a speech topic and prepare three visual aids, each of a different type, for use with the speech. Complete a Visual Aid Check List (in Appendix E) on each of the three visual aids.

2. From one of your speeches used during the semester, take one of the major points and attempt to support this with a variety of different types of visual aids. You should create at least three different types to support the same point. Prepare each visual aid on an 8½ × 11 sheet of paper and submit these to your instructor with a completed Visual Aid Check List. Identify type of material and size you would use if presenting this in an average size classroom.

3. Taking the following set of information, present this data by using at least three different types of visual aids. Prepare each visual aid on an 8½ × 11 sheet of paper (but indicate type of material and size you would use if presenting this in a normal size classroom) and submit these to your instructor.

    The CCC Book Publishing Company sold 10,000 copies of one of its recent publications. Sales of the book were distributed as follows:
    >   1500 copies sold retail by mail orders at $9.95
    >   1000 copies to high school libraries at $6.95
    >   1400 copies to college libraries at $6.95
    >   1800 copies to public libraries at $6.95
    >   1300 copies to bookstores at $6.50
    >   3000 copies to wholesale jobbers at $6.00

    Complete a Visual Aid Check List (Appendix E) on each visual aid you develop.

Listening
to Speeches*

$\mathscr{H}$ 7

*By Carl Kell.

OBJECTIVES ∾

After completing this chapter, you should be able to:

1. *Understand* the general objectives of listening training.
2. *Understand* the "thought speed" problem in listening comprehension.
3. *Understand* the differences between the good listener and the poor listener.
4. Continually *improve* your listening skills both in class and out of class.

A central principle of contemporary speech communication theory affirms the shared responsibility of a speaker and listener for an effective communication experience. In the public speaking situation the listener should not be perceived as a vessel for the speaker to fill. The beginning student speaker should be primarily concerned with utilizing the skills of effective listening to be better able to "read" his audience, improve his speaking skills, and finally, be a more sensitive listener to the communications of others. This chapter examines the principles of listening training as the key to improving skills in public and interpersonal speech communication.

Scholars in speech communication agreed long ago that "listening . . . is a much more complex process than the mere reception of an identifiable signal."[1] Indeed, the listening pro-

---

[1]Wayne Thompson, *Quantitative Research in Public Address and Communication* (New York: Random House, 1967), p. 131.

cess is as widely misunderstood and as complex to master as any other element in the speech communication process. To illustrate this for yourself, answer the following eleven true-false questions concerning the listening process.

T F 1. Listening is largely a matter of intelligence.
T F 2. Speaking is a more important part of the communication process than listening.
T F 3. Listening requires little energy; it is "easy."
T F 4. Listening is an automatic, involuntary reflex.
T F 5. Speakers can command listening to occur within an audience.
T F 6. Hearing ability significantly determines listening ability.
T F 7. The speaker is totally responsible for the success of communication.
T F 8. People listen every day. This daily practice eliminates the need for listening training.
T F 9. Competence in listening develops naturally.
T F 10. When you learned to read, you simultaneously learned to listen.
T F 11. Listening is only a matter of understanding the words of the speaker.[2]

If you answered any of the questions *true*, this chapter can provide a realistic understanding of the nature of listening and its importance in communication, for every question in the test is *false*! (Even if you answered all of the questions *false*, you might still read the chapter.)

Listening most certainly stands as the most "taken for granted" element in the speech communication process. One survey of communication showed that listening is the communication activity engaged in most frequently.[3] Because listening is such an important form of verbal communication, you

[2]Larry Barker, *Listening Behavior* (Englewood Cliffs, N.J.: Prentice-Hall, 1971), p. xiii.
[3]Paul Tory Rankin, "The Measurement of the Ability to Understand Spoken Language" (unpublished Ph. D. dissertation, University of Michigan, 1926).

need to acquire and practice effective listening skills to: (1) meet the communication needs present in everyday life for effective interaction; and (2) improve your speech communication abilities. But, *wanting* to become an effective listener-communicator is the first step in establishing personal skills in the speech communication process.

What is "listening"? The process has been defined as "the selective process of attending to, hearing, understanding, and remembering aural symbols."[4] Thus, listening involves four separate, but interrelated, processes. *Attention* refers to focusing perception on visual and/or verbal stimuli (the speaker's message); *hearing* refers to the physiological process of receiving aural stimuli; *understanding* refers to assigning meaning to messages received (similar meaning, it is hoped, to that intended by the initiator of the message); and *remembering* involves the storing of meaningful information in the mind for the purpose of recalling it at a later time.[5]

Listening has been shown to be strongly correlated to intelligence, scholastic aptitude, verbal aptitude, and vocabulary. Listening is also related to a person's general inclination to be self-motivated in communicative situations: "real interest in the subject discussed," "emotional adjustment to the speaker's thesis," "ability to see significance in the subject discussed," and "curiosity about the subject discussed."[6] The listening process requires, therefore, four basic mental abilities and a degree of real effort on the receiver's part during the time he is receiving the message.[7]

It is easy but usually unfair to engage a person in conversation or listen to a speech or lecture with no expectation of learning anything new. Assume an attitude of *positive regard* for every person. How do they feel? Why are they saying what they are saying? The task of the listener is to *look for* the communicative "worth" of the other person. Every interaction, conversa-

[4]Barker, *Listening Behavior*, p. 17.
[5]Ibid.
[6]Thompson, *Quantitative Research in Public Address and Communication*, pp. 140, 147.
[7]Ibid.

tion, and speech has some kind of purpose. Assume the duty you have as a sensitive communicator is to be in the proper frame of "attitude" toward the other person. You may even find more pleasure in the communication of others than you find in your own remarks.

Too often the best behavior we exhibit as a listener is mere superficiality. Avoid the tendency to spread your eye contact and interests over the entire communication landscape. Focus your attention and interest, your eye contact, even your "body lean" toward the speaker. Listening should be a natural blend of nonverbal and verbal purposive attention and expression that encourages the other party to enjoy his interpersonal encounter or public speech with you or to do his best in his public speaking with you as a member of his audience.

The major problem that short-circuits our day-to-day listening pattern is *thought speed.* Central to this problem are the disparities between listening speed and speech speed. The average person speaks at a rate of 125–175 words per minute. However, college students have been tested by means of electronically compressed audio taped passages; these tests show that with little or no practice, these students maintain 80 to 100 percent comprehension at double normal speaking rate. Consequently, it is fairly certain that most individuals could easily digest compressed speech at an approximate rate of 400 words per minute with their usual comprehension. This relationship between listening speed rate and speech speed rate reveals an obvious problem. In normal day-to-day interpersonal communication, listeners commonly take "mental vacations" during the "left-over" time. Only practice at using the extra time properly can correct this problem. Professor J. Vernon Jensen suggests the following ways to use "left-over" time to advantage:

1. *Determine the speaker's purpose.* Is he primarily attempting to teach (informative purpose), or influence the attitudes, beliefs, or behavior patterns of his listeners (persuasive purpose)? In either case the listener must "ask" the speaker— "What is it you want us to know?" and "What is it you want us to do?"

2. *Determine the major ideas.* In either of the two lines of analysis (persuasive or informative) the speaker will bluntly or inferentially "signpost" his main points. On the one hand, he will say "my first point is . . ." or "the central issue is . . ." or use some other strong transitional bridge to get you set to listen to a major block of subpoints and details in his speech. On the other hand, the beginning speaker (and, at times, the mature speaker) may leave traces of main points, either because he won't work at the task of speech construction or because he disdains the fundamentals of speech construction in lieu of conveying an "educated" analysis. In either case, the listener must exert a real effort to structure the speech for his own well-being. It is equally easy to assume you have heard the main points when you really haven't. However, the real work involved is always worth the listener's efforts.

3. *Seek out the organizational pattern.* It is equally worth the listener's effort to perceive and recognize the speaker's structural pattern of speech development. Current research corroborates the scholarship on organization and listening; that is, concentrating on organization and ideas is significantly linked to effective listening. Indeed, to determine that the speaker's organization is chronological, spatial, cause-to-effect, or any other special format is a meaningful task for the listener. However, as Jensen points out, speeches with poor (or no) organization may still offer an interesting analysis.

4. *Recognize significant details.* Important facts, stories, survey results, and other types of data used in the speech may help the listener retain the main points of the speech. Of course, the speaker should assist his audience by showing the relationship between statements and the attention support material. Obviously, many student speakers, and adult speakers for that matter, simply do not give their audiences such organizational cues in order for the listener to follow the arguments.[8]

[8]J. Vernon Jensen, *Perspectives in Oral Communication* (Boston: Holbrook Press, Inc., 1970), p. 122 ff.

Another problem that short-circuits listening skills results from overreacting emotionally to the elements of a message. Nichols and Stevens noted that listeners actually stop listening when they overreact to such jargon terms as *pervert, fink, mod, beat, cool, hippie,* and *Black Power.*[9] Make your own list of terms that involve strong emotions and produce poor listening. Obviously, we listen to those ideas that are best aligned with our general or specific world view while screening out other ideas that don't mesh with our attitudes and opinions.

Griffin and Patton have stated two additional general problems that stifle effective listening: *a tendency to evaluate a message prematurely,* and *difficulty in distinguishing between observational statements and statements of inference.* In the first case, one impairs the process of reception if one decides too early that the speaker has very little to say. Too often, one renders a judgment before the message is completed. In the second case, one must never confuse observation with inference. For instance, just because the interstate gas sign is visible from long distances doesn't mean that a gas station is in operation or that the station is even open. Everyone has had this kind of experience, and has experienced such problems in "short-circuiting" the listening process.

Effective listening is a complex, but not impossible, task. The following list compares effective and ineffective listening.[10] Evaluate your own responses.

The Good Listener	*The Poor Listener*
1. Receives both verbal and nonverbal communication.	1. Regards the topic itself as boring and uninteresting.
2. Sees and feels as well as hears.	2. Gets sidetracked by criticizing delivery and vocabulary.

[9]Ralph Nichols and L. A. Stevens, *Are You Listening?* (New York: McGraw-Hill, 1957), pp. 90–94.

[10]William K. Amiott, *Grouping For Solution* (Sigma Nu Inc., Educational Foundation, 1971), p. 18.

3. Is able to separate visual and emotional cues.

3. Becomes overexcited and distracted by part of the message.

4. Checks back with the speaker for clarification.

4. Listens only for cold, hard fact and misses all other cues.

5. Works to improve communication skills.

5. Insists on outlining everything in his mind.

6. Actually saves time through listening efficiently.

6. Hides boredom by carefully faking attention.

7. Avoids unnecessary disagreement, misunderstanding and repetition.

7. Relaxes by allowing himself to follow distractions.

8. Enhances the self-image of the speaker.

8. Evades concentrating on topics that are difficult.

9. Is eager and unhurried, not "putting off" the speaker.

9. Reacts internally to any emotionally loaded word.

10. Is tolerant of opinions inconsistent with his or her own.

10. Wastes thought power pondering inconsequential matters.

We have pointed out that the listener to speech communication is as responsible for the results of a message as the sender of the message. The statement certainly wasn't meant to be a flippant attention-getting device. Central to your growth and development in this speech communication course is becoming an evaluative, helping listener, improving your own communication as you help improve the communication of other students. A superior class in speech communication is marked by a pervasive attitude of critical listening and helpful commentary on *all* assignments by every member of the class.

Summary

Speakers and listeners share responsibility for effective communication. Effective listening is good training for effective speaking. Listening involves four processes: attention, hearing, understanding, and remembering.

One can improve listening behavior through various methods: determining the speaker's purpose, determining the major ideas, recognizing the speaker's organizational pattern, and recognizing significant details.

Effective listening can be stifled through overuse of emotional jargon, premature evaluation of a message, and confusion between observation and inference. Effective speech communication behavior combines a knowledgeable awareness of the mechanics of the art as well as a genuine sensitivity to the human elements of the art. Listening effectiveness is the key that unlocks the door to your personal communication improvement.

EXERCISES ❧

1. Listen to a public speech outside the classroom and compare written notes with a classmate as to main theme, main points, type of organization, and types of argument. Obviously, you will want to look for and raise questions about points of difference.

2. In contemporary America, any semester of college experience has election year situations; local, state, or national. Search for a public political speech event that you can attend either live or through the mass media. Compare your analysis of the speech with that of your friends or the press.

3. As an in-class discussion, exchange views on the best and worst communications you know. Compile your individual lists into two major lists on the blackboard, then analyze the dimension of *listening* involved. The entire chapter could serve as a background for this particular assignment.

4. To test your listening abilities concerning statements of fact and statements of inference, take the following test. Read the story only *once* (if done as an oral assignment read the story aloud only *once*) and answer the questions as quickly as possible. (The answers can be found on page 145.)

The Story

A businessman had just turned off the lights in the store when a man appeared and demanded money. The owner opened a cash register. The contents of the cash register were scooped up, and the man sped away. A member of the police force was notified promptly.

Statements About the Story

T F ? 1. A man appeared after the owner had turned off his store lights.

T F ? 2. The robber was a man.

T F ? 3. The man did not demand money.

T F ? 4. The man who opened the cash register was the owner.

T F ? 5. The storeowner scooped up the contents of the cash register and ran away.

T F ? 6. Someone opened a cash register.

T F ? 7. After the man who demanded the money scooped up the contents of the cash register, he ran away.

T F ? 8. While the cash register contained money, the story does not state how much.

T F ? 9. The robber demanded money of the owner.

T F ? 10. The story concerns a series of events in which only three persons were referred to: the owner of the store, a man who demanded money, and a member of the police force.

Answers

(T) F ? 1. A man appeared after the owner (business-man—not necessarily owner) had turned off his store lights.

T (F) ? 2. The robber was a man. (Do not *know* he was a *robber*.)

(T) F ? 3. The man did not demand money.

T (F) ? 4. The *man* who opened the cash register was the owner. (Owner could have been a woman.)

T (F) ? 5. The store owner scooped up the contents of the cash register and ran away. (Doesn't say *who* scooped up contents.)

T F (?) 6. Someone opened a cash register. (*Owner* opened cash register—this is debatable because owner is *someone*.)

T (F) ? 7. After the man who demanded the money scooped up the contents of the cash register, he ran away. (Doesn't say man who demanded money is same person who scooped up contents.)

T (F) ?   8. While the cash register contained money, the story does not state how much. (The *contents* were scooped up—doesn't say money.)

T F (?)   9. The robber demanded money of the owner. (Doesn't say—it says *a* man demanded money—could have been other than man who ran away, etc.)

T F (?) 10. The story concerns a series of events in which only three persons were referred to: the owner of the store, a man who demanded money, and a member of the police force. (Businessman?)

Developing Persuasive Speech*

✱ 8

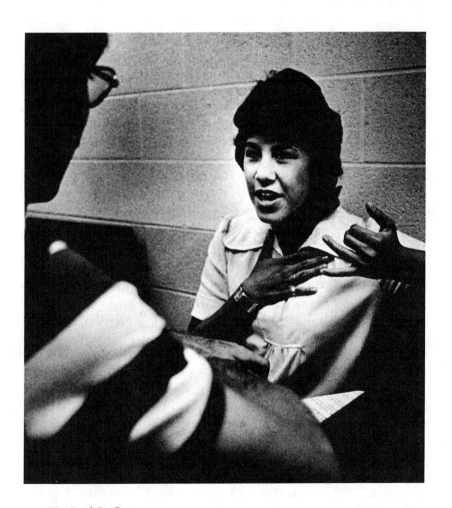

*By Paul R. Corts.

OBJECTIVES ୯ଛ

After completing this chapter, you should be able to:

1. *Be aware of* the role of persuasion as one type of public speech communication in society.
2. *Be aware of* the need to use persuasion responsibly.
3. *Prepare* the content of a persuasive speech.
4. *Identify* appropriate research techniques for development of persuasive speech content.
5. *Identify* types of supporting material for use in a persuasive speech.
6. *Identify* and *create* forms of proof for use in a persuasive speech.

With the possible exceptions of sleeping and eating, most people spend more time persuading than any other single activity. Our history can be clearly seen in a gentle tracing of controversy. From the trivial question of the cave man pondering whether to try a new meat or not, to the more serious question of the twentieth century—should oleo be colored yellow like butter—man's history has been one of resolving controversy. From these light decisions to more meaningful questions such as the question faced by Adam when tempted by Eve (or Eve when tempted by the Serpent), or who should rule and who should be ruled, or should laws restricting marijuana be abolished—our history and our contemporary world are made up largely of perplexing questions with staunch advocates propounding their persuasion.

In some ways it is difficult, if not impossible, to speak without attempting to persuade. Some define communication as persuasion. From the point of view that to say anything is to urge that thing to be accepted (heard and considered), all speech is persuasion. But in a deeper sense, you are forced into situations every day when you must use your best persuasion. Defending your point of view in the classroom is persuasion. Presenting support for your own personal beliefs is persuasion. And every lover knows that every reservoir of charm turned on to the love partner is persuasion.

Of course there are other ways to solve controversy. The police officer may call out to the accused: "Stop or I'll shoot!" to resolve the controversy of whether the accused should be arrested and tried. Persuasion is not the only means of solving controversy. In the operation of government and in the managing of individual lives, persuasion is only one means of solving problems.

Throughout history one of the frequently used methods of resolving controversy has been authority. You probably experienced the use of authority for decision-making in your own life when Mom or Dad laid down the absolute law.

Authoritarian methods for enforcing decisions include force, moral suasion, or propaganda. Force is a crude method which subdues objection and thought by physical strength. As long as you possess the greatest physical strength, this can appear to be a satisfactory method; however, the force method is juxtaposed to the view of humans as rational beings. Moral suasion relies on societal and peer group pressures to bring about acceptance to authoritarian decisions. The "threat" of a grade in this class is sufficient moral suasion to make you conform to "authoritarian" requirements of this course because various social pressures exist to encourage you to attend class and perform successfully. Propaganda is another authoritarian method which circumvents the rational thought process to produce voluntary acceptance of authoritarian decrees. These authoritarian methods have been frequently exhibited in government, religious movements, social and fraternal organizations, business operations, and even in family and personal relationships.

Another method of solving problems is known as the "reflection" method. Through the process of lengthy reflection on a problem by all parties concerned, one can eventually find a solution which will be acceptable to all. Unless a person, organization, subgroup, or society is completely devoted to a rational, cooperative, unbiased, sober process, this method cannot work.

Another possible method of decision-making is persuasion, a democratic process. Decisions arrived at through the process of persuasion may not contain absolute truth, but they should provide a decision which is the most wise, feasible, and pragmatic for the moment. Persuasion allows for all views to be expressed and for society to chart its own course. Someone has said: "The public may not know enough to be experts but they know enough to judge between them." Theoretically, this is the way our government should function; ideally, this is the method our society should use in decision-making. But there are weaknesses in every method of decision-making, and as a consequence, the various methods are used in differing degrees at different times. However, persuasion pervades the other processes, as an element of persuasion can be seen in each of these methods: consequently, persuasion seems to be the most important method. This is our reason for studying it—to help you become a more effective participant in life, which is in many ways a continuous process of decision-making.

Responsible Persuasion

The process of persuasion carries with it the awesome subject of free speech. Persuasion can only work in a framework that provides for freedom of speech. This precious right, always under fire from radicals of every walk, is often taken for granted in America—but only the naive can consider it a certainty and only the naive can cling to it ideally. Whether you consider yourself radical right or radical left or somewhere in between, you personally should recognize your right to speak as well as cherish that right for others, remembering that defending a person's right to speak does not carry an endorsement of his point of view. It should also be noted that the right to speak does not include the right to be taken seriously. Ed Howe, an American journalist at the turn of the century, once said: "I express many absurd opinions, but I am not the first man to do it: American freedom consists largely in talking nonsense." The point is that you have the right of free expression of that "nonsense."

One of the awesome responsibilities for every speaker, especially every public speaker, is to consider seriously the content of what he or she is saying. As Mark Twain put it: "In our country we have those three unspeakably precious things: freedom of speech, freedom of conscience, and the prudence never to practice either." There may be times when suppression of your own free speech will be deemed in the best interests at the moment.

Finally, there are some legal restrictions to complete free speech. It seems obvious that total ideal free speech cannot function in a highly organized, complex, and vast society. It may well suffer breakdown in the smallest, most tightly knit group. It is your responsibility as a citizen to exercise your rights within the framework, striving always to keep the limitations to a minimum. America's will to protect freedom of speech has been and is being tested. It is our duty to continue in the American tradition to exercise this right in a responsible yet vigorous way.

Audience Analysis and Adaptation

Having established a topic for your persuasive speech (refer to Chapter 3), your next big hurdle is to "prove" your point! When you are presenting a *speech in which you are attempting to change the attitude, opinion, or action of the audience,* the audience will typically be asking for a basis for accepting the substance of your speech. Thus the audience is a crucial factor in the development of any speech and will be the practical judge of your success at persuasion.

When you present a speech, consider the issue or topic of that speech in the context of the speech situation rather than in the context of creating a literary work in a vacuum. This is one of the most significant differences between preparing a speech and writing an essay. A speech has a spontaneous quality because it is directed to a specific audience at a specific time and will most likely receive a specific response. The essay deals with less specific circumstances and a more unknown audience.

It is the speaker's responsibility to evaluate the audience. Typically a speaker should know the wants, needs, and values held by the audience as individuals and as a collective group. Often this judgment can be made in a general way based on recognizable observations such as age or dress, and general information such as educational level, religious background, social status, or occupation.

Determining the wants, needs, and values of your audience does not mean that you should take a poll of the audience and then develop a speech to satisfy the audience. This is not persuasion but rather reinforcement. Knowing how your audience perceives issues and topics will help you adjust your presentation to downplay differences between speaker and audience and give preference to the similarities between speaker and audience. People respond differently to issues, and most people will readily accept the idea of varying viewpoints. These people, often referred to as "open-minded," are fair, and they are willing to put personal views to the test against opposing views. They will give your views a hearing if you present your ideas in the context of a search for the most practical solution or the most workable approach.

Supporting Material

No matter what you choose as a topic for a persuasive speech, rarely will you be expert enough to deal with the issue without researching. Researching in this sense really means finding available data that relate directly to your topic. Such data are referred to as "supporting material" because you will use it as the basis for developing your topic. As in any building situation, the completed structure is only as strong as its foundation. By starting with an adequate supply of carefully gleaned supporting material, the speaker can proceed to develop a convincing speech. (Review Chapter 3.)

There is more to developing a persuasive speech than collecting a massive amount of data and throwing it into a big collection called a "speech," but the art of collecting data is a first step. You know the saying that there are two sides to every issue, and there is usually abundant supporting material for both sides. The more serious effort is not finding data but using the data. In this chapter the types of supporting material essential for a beginning persuasive speaker are identified.

Proofs

First we should consider *proofs,* which can be divided into two broad categories: *artistic* and *non-artistic.* Artistic proofs are those types of support for a speech which a speaker develops creatively and are usually referred to as emotional (pathos) and ethical (ethos) proofs. Non-artistic proofs are already available types of support but require research, location, and investigation and are usually referred to as logical (logos) proofs.

Non-artistic Proofs

Because they are more concrete, recognizable, and easier for the beginning student to work with, let us consider non-artistic proofs first. This type of supporting material can be classified into four basic types: *statistical information, expert and lay opinion (quotations), specific example, and anecdotes (illustration).*

First, a student will usually think of statistical information since this is the type of data that pops into most of our minds when we think about "getting some facts" for a speech. *Statistical information* as used here *refers to quantifiable data* and can be a very strong type of supporting material. If the data come from reliable sources, by their nature statistics cannot be challenged as easily as other forms of supporting material except in their interpretation.

A second major category of supporting material is quotation. *Quotations are statements made by experts and lay people on the issues at hand.* Quite often a student researching for a speech will be frustrated to find that there are about as many positions as there are people; but only some of these positions can be blended into the position advocated by the speaker. One of the most important things to remember when locating quotations to use in your speech is to be certain of the acceptability of the author of the quotations. It will do little good to find a quotation that says precisely what you want in support of your speech if the author of the quotation is an unacceptable source for your audience. The force of a quotation lies in its acceptability, and its acceptability will be determined by whether the audience perceives the maker of the quotation as an expert or reliable source.

Another form of supporting material is the specific example. *A specific example can be defined as a real life experience which exemplifies the position in question.* If you can take an occurrence from real life which bears directly on this issue of your speech, then you have strong support for your speech because this example has been drawn from the tests of reality. Unlike a statistic which is open to many confusing interpretations, and unlike a quotation in which the reliability of the author of the quotation can often be questioned, a real life experience is more readily accepted by most audiences. Frequently you can find specific examples in the general reading which you will be doing in preparation for your speech. Often you may recall occurrences in your own life experience which will be appropriate. These experiences from either source are equally acceptable for use in a speech.

Another type of supporting material is the anecdote or illustration. This may be humorous, although it does not have to be. *An anecdote is a fabricated story or a contrived example to illustrate a real point.* It is similar to a specific example because it should have its basis in fact, but there is usually less authenticity attached to an anecdote or illustration. The specific example is usually more directly to the point, while the anecdote or illustration tends to be a longer elaboration with more detail about a real, partially real, or make-believe event. The anecdote allows the speaker to use creative imagination in developing factual supporting material rather than simply using the material or information of others. When using such supporting material, you might want to introduce the material by saying "Suppose, . . ." or "Imagine, if you will, . . ." or similar statements to alert the audience that the material may not be entirely factual.

The following rules apply in using supportive material:

1. *Be certain that the supporting material used is relevant to your speech.* Typically a beginning speech student will find information that bears on the topic generally rather than specifically. In a quest for using a sufficient amount of supporting material, a student will often indiscriminately use supporting material that is not directly supportive of the position advocated in the speech. Check and recheck to make certain that the material that you are using is the best possible material available to support the specific issue which you are dealing with in your speech.

2. *Be as direct as possible.* Especially in the use of statistics brevity can be easily accomplished; but you should avoid long lists of statistics because a large amount of numbers or the repeated use of numbers can be confusing to the audience and will seriously affect its ability to follow you or to recall the data or even the major issues of the speech. In developing quotations from expert and lay opinion, some beginning speakers have a tendency to quote too extensively. Be on your guard to make your quotations as direct and to the point as possible.

3. *Use a variety of types of supporting material.* The typical beginning speaker will simply find a collection of items which could be used to support the speech and will indiscriminately use these support items without considering the variety of supporting material being used. The effective speaker, however, will carefully choose supporting material based upon its type of classification to make certain that all types of supporting material are being used and that the

speech is not becoming bogged down with an abundance of one particular type. Variety is the crucial element, and the beginning speaker should carefully guard against monotony in the use of types of supporting material.

Artistic Proofs

Artistic proofs must also be considered by the student speaker. A good speech is supported by "facts and figures"; but audiences consider much more than that in deciding whether to accept a speaker's point of view. You may have heard a person react to a highly logical speech filled with specific supporting data by saying: "What the speaker says may be true, but I still don't accept it!" Why does a person react to a speech in this way?

As discussed earlier in this chapter, people base their beliefs, attitudes, and opinions on subjective, sometimes unexamined, suppositions and judgments and on their own personal wants, needs, and desires. Thus much more is involved in persuasion than the mere arrangement of non-artistic supporting material. Creative and artistic proof is required. Even supporting material can be artistically created, such as in the case of a contrived illustration or imaginative anecdote, but artistic proof deals specifically with issues of emotional and ethical proof.

Emotional proof, which is traditionally referred to as pathos, is the use of words, illustrations, or other material which make an impact on a person's feeling and thus affect physical and mental responses. This is a bona fide form of proof. Many students shy away from use of emotional proof for fear of being branded as a nonlogical speaker. Unable to picture yourself as such an orator, you may wish to shun any consideration of emotional proof. But human character compels us to act and make final judgments, to varying degrees, on the basis of emotional considerations or the "feelings" which we have. You should not appeal exclusively to emotion, just as an audience should not render a judgment based solely on emotional reaction. Proper use of creative emotional proof occurs when you present logical supporting material to substantiate a point and then embellish the logical point with emotional proof. This can be accomplished, for example, when you present a point of view, use sound logical supporting material to "prove" the point, use emotionally charged words (see Chapter 4 on language), and use a human or personal illustration, all of which should be unified with the aim of affecting the "feeling" of the listener in relation to the audience's needs, wants, and desires.

You should also be aware of ethical proof (ethos) and its potential in persuasion. *Ethical proof is the support that a person receives because of believability.* This believability (or credibility) is something which can be left to chance, but a speaker should take the responsibility to develop this proof. In general, people react positively or negatively to others on the basis of a variety of criteria. This spontaneous reaction which the audience has toward you the speaker may greatly influence whether the audience will accept your logical and emotional proof.

This ethical proof inherent in the speaker has been frequently referred to as "image" in contemporary political campaigning. Certainly, image is at issue but ethical proof should not be viewed as only a cosmetic. A speaker can do a great deal to create the impression of honesty, integrity, sincerity, and other traits that he actually possesses. Ancient writers on the subject of good speech communication perceived the need for a highly moral quality in an effective speaker. "A good speaker," the ancients agreed, "is a *good man* speaking well." The emphasis here is on the *good man* in the context of the society making the judgment. A speaker who is genuinely and innately a "good man" will be more readily perceived as a "good man" and will therefore be more effective than the speaker who does not make the favorable impression. In addition, because the power of persuasion is great, the training of a speaker should carry with it concern for integrity, honesty, and other virtues of the moral man.

Whatever you can do to make yourself more believable as an authority will pay off for you in your success as a speaker. Some general guidelines of helpful ways of increasing your believability are:

1. Conduct yourself physically in a manner appropriate with the setting and occasion.

2. Demonstrate your grasp of the issues by indicating your personal experience or the extent of your research.
3. Demonstrate your fairness in examining all sides of the question.
4. Show respect for alternate points of view.
5. Indicate the motivation for your position on the issue.

These same considerations should be made by each member of the audience to be an effective listener.

To help you grasp the use of supporting material in a speech, Figure 8.1 presents a student speech and a student's analysis of the speech. This will show you how one speaker used a variety of types of supporting material effectively to prove the point of the speech.

Summary

The public speaker disseminates information and attempts to change attitude, opinion, or belief. This is a part of our democratic society and the tradition of the American system. It is not something to be shunned, but is rather something to be understood. You are encouraged to become skilled in its use so that you can be a full-fledged participating member of the American system.

To achieve success in the dissemination of information and the changing of people's attitudes, opinions, or beliefs, it is important to build a speech with substantive support. Your speech should have a broad general heading with its development demonstrated by three to five essential subpoints. Each of the subpoints should have "supporting material" in the nature of statistics, quotations, specific examples, and anecdotes or illustrations. A speaker should use emotional and ethical proof in support of the speech.

Research your topic well, moving from general background information to very specific information. You should liberally and systematically record your material for best results in using the material to develop a good speech.

Figure 8.1

Student Analysis

Uses two personal experiences to introduce topic. They are realistic enough to gain attention and yet surprising enough to arouse interest toward causes and solutions.

Ethical appeals supporting speaker credibility through personal examples

Student Speech

YOUR FRIENDLY NEIGHBORHOOD MECHANIC*

Deadra Longworth

Mankato State University

Mankato, Minnesota

Coached by Larry Schnoor

Last March while driving home on Interstate 80, I suddenly realized that even though I was applying pressure to my gas pedal, I was going nowhere. Fortunately, I was able to pull off the freeway, down an exit ramp and anxiously into an awaiting service station. After the mechanic checked the car over, he assured me, "Don't worry little lady, you only have a broken fan belt." Well, this "little lady" left Iowa owing a bill of $85.00 for the replacement of that broken fan belt.

Last October 23, I rode with a group of students to Omaha, Nebraska, in a large van. Later that evening as one of the students was returning home from his night on the town, he suddenly lost his ability to shift. He was lucky that he was not injured, but his speed was slow enough so he could pull off to the side of the road and wait to be towed to a garage. Believe me, it was difficult for him to accept the bill of $375.00 when you consider that just a week before he had paid $285.00 for a new rebuilt transmission.

*Reprinted from *Winning Orations* (Mankato, Minnesota: The Interstate Oratorical Association, 1976).

Student Analysis

Student Speech

Student Analysis	Student Speech
Transition →	*Instances like this can happen to anybody at any time, but both of my cases involve a common denomination: auto repair incompetency and fraud.*
Rhetorical questions are then asked for application of problems to the audience. It might stimulate the listeners to think of other similar personal experiences which yielded a comparable result.	*When was the last time you had your car in the garage for repairs? Were you pleased with the work that was done? Do you believe you were treated honestly and fairly? That the price you were charged was relatively just? Well if you were, please leave me the name of the mechanic. Unfortunately, most of us leave these service stations feeling totally frustrated and upset.*
Problem → Good contrast between "dream" and "nightmare."	*Owning an automobile may be the American dream, but keeping it repaired has become the American nightmare.*
Introduces three problem areas. →	*Supplementing every man's personal experience, evidence exists to show that the incompetency and fraud of the Auto Repair Industry can no longer be ignored and that steps must be taken to correct this abuse of the driving public. This abuse involves inflated costs, deceitful practices, and inexcusable incompetency.*
Problems A. Inflated Costs Expert Opinion → Statistics →	*Popular Science states that last year inadequate auto repair was the leading consumer complaint in America, and Margaret Carlson, former research associate for the Center of Auto Safety, states in her book, How to Get Your Car Repaired Without Getting Gypped, that Americans spend over 29 billion dollars a year on servicing and repair. Yet 11 billion or almost half, is spent on shoddy, unneeded, and over priced repairs.*
Transition → B. Fraud	*Now, many bad repairs can be attributed to incompetency, but plenty are outrageous frauds that contribute heavily to that wasted 11 billion a year.*

Student Analysis

Student Speech

Automotive transmissions capable of running 150,000 miles with relatively little maintenance seem to be the most popular target of the dishonest mechanic. In a recent crackdown on transmission rip-offs, the U.S. Attorney's office in Washington D.C. uncovered a modus operandi typical of many crooked shops. It goes like this: After having

→ Expert Opinion

seen an ad in the newspaper for a special on transmission repairs, we take our car to the garage complaining of a little transmission trouble.

→ Hypothetical Illustration

The mechanic then takes it apart. Now the diagnosis may vary, but the price is usually about the same. Somewhere between $200 and $300 dollars. Well, after your cardiac arrest, you may decide you'd like to take your car to another shop for another opinion. The mechanic then informs you he's sorry, but he'll have to charge you at least $75 dollars or leave your transmission in pieces on the garage floor. At this point, you've been taken for at least $75 dollars. Should you decide to have it repaired at this shop—beware! The mechanic may make a needed adjustment, paint your transmission, and charge you about $300 dollars for a new one, or he can do something as simple as replacing a $20.00 vacuum modulator and charge you $225 dollars for a new rebuilt transmission. However done, it all adds up to a very profitable service.

→ Transition

Automotive transmissions may be the most popular area of deceitful practices, but unfortunately, they are not the only ones. Many frauds are worked when you simply leave your car at a service station unattended, or step away to buy a soft drink. That's when the greedy operator has ample opportunity to pull one or more wires so the trouble lights go on or the car won't start.

Student Analysis

Student Speech

Expert Opinion →

Specific Examples →

Changing Times, June 1974, tells of one technically minded bandit who was known to spray titanium tetrachloride, a colorless liquid that creates a dense white smoke onto the alternator of cars. This successfully scared the wits and dollars out of many unsuspecting motorists. Another was known to pour common soda pop into the batteries of cars which made them foam profusely—another sale!

Transition →

C. Incompetency

Unfortunately, the questionable practices that many mechanics use to earn that extra buck are not at all uncommon. What I find more alarming is that many more mechanics are guilty of incompetency, and this incompetency is dangerous.

Statistics →
Emotional Appeal →

Last year, for every 1,000 fatal accidents reviewed, 17 percent were the direct result of inadequate auto repair. Yet, daily, we deliver into these so-called technicians' hands, millions of incredibly complex machines in need of maintenance and repair.

Expert Opinion →
Statistics →

Donald Randare, Washington based attorney and author of the book, The Great American Auto Repair Robbery, tells us that of the nation's 900 thousand auto mechanics, less than 40 percent have been classified as skilled labor by the Bureau of Census. The competency of the Auto Repair Industry leaves a great deal to be desired.

Expert Opinion →

Statistics →

A recent study, conducted by the Highway Safety Institute at the University of Michigan, established the chances of the average motorist receiving a proper headlight adjustment, even when the mechanic was using headlight aiming equipment, at only about 50 percent. Of the more difficult jobs, the Institute estimated probability of correctness to be one in three.

This is not an isolated example.

Student Analysis

Student Speech

Expert Opinion

Statistics

Internal summary
Transition

Solution
External (What government agencies and others can do.)

Emotional Appeal

Expert Opinion

Statistics

The Automobile Club of Missouri recently reviewed some 6,500 repairs that had been recommended by its St. Louis Diagnostic Center. Less than 65 percent of all the repairs reviewed, which had been completed by various shops and mechanics, were judged competent, safe, or even minimally satisfactory. What is worse is that 17 percent of the brake work was judged dangerous.

As examples and statistics pile up, it becomes evident that in an industry so inseparably connected with the motorist's economic interests as well as our own personal safety and survival, there is a colossal need for some procedure which can assure the public that the shops offering the needed repairs at least possess the minimum performance capabilities to undertake those repairs they offer to sell the public.

I find it quite ironic; we require careful registration, education and licensing of such professions as barbers and beauticians, but of a profession so vital to our everyday existence, we do not even require certification of competency.

As early as 1970, the Automobile Dealers Association and the four auto manufacturers realized the seriousness of this problem and formed a non-profit organization called the National Institute of Automotive Service Excellence. The sole responsibility of this organization was to develop a program in which mechanics employed in servicing and repairs can obtain certification indicating they have achieved specific levels of competency in all areas. Unfortunately, this program was implemented on only a voluntary basis. Of the 900 thousand automobile mechanics in the Nation, less that 20 thousand have taken and completed all 8 of the competency tests.

Student Analysis

Internal summary

Transition

Internal (What we can do.)

Signposts

Summary
and
Motivation

Student Speech

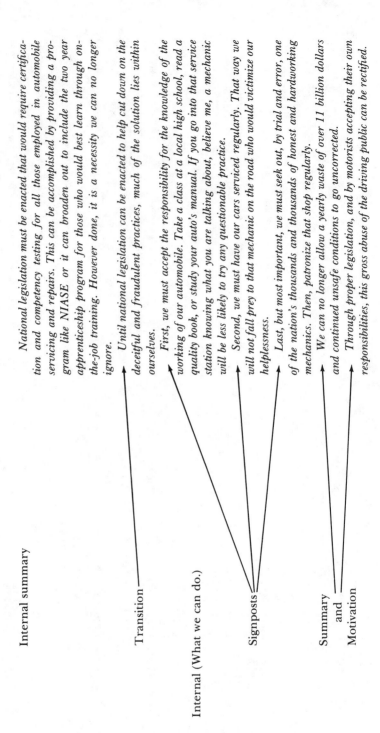

National legislation must be enacted that would require certification and competency testing for all those employed in automobile servicing and repairs. This can be accomplished by providing a program like NIASE or it can broaden out to include the two year apprenticeship program for those who would best learn through on-the-job training. However done, it is a necessity we can no longer ignore.

Until national legislation can be enacted to help cut down on the deceitful and fraudulent practices, much of the solution lies within ourselves.

First, we must accept the responsibility for the knowledge of the working of our automobile. Take a class at a local high school, read a quality book, or study your auto's manual. If you go into that service station knowing what you are talking about, believe me, a mechanic will be less likely to try any questionable practice.

Second, we must have our cars serviced regularly. That way we will not fall prey to that mechanic on the road who would victimize our helplessness.

Last, but most important, we must seek out, by trial and error, one of the nation's thousands and thousands of honest and hardworking mechanics. Then, patronize that shop regularly.

We can no longer allow a yearly waste of over 11 billion dollars and continued unsafe conditions to go uncorrected.

Through proper legislation, and by motorists accepting their own responsibilities, this gross abuse of the driving public can be rectified.

EXERCISES ❧

1. Take one of the major points you have used in one of your speeches for this course. Develop three different types of supporting material for the major point and label each type. Use the "Major Point Development Form" in Appendix F to complete this assignment.

2. Using the following set of information, create two distinct artistic proofs. Try to "prove" that the company should or should not shift emphasis in its advertising budget.

   The CCC Book Publishing Company has published 20,000 copies of a particular book. The advertising budget for this book was:

Advertising aimed at General Public	$400
Advertising aimed at Libraries	$275
Advertising aimed at Wholesalers	$375

   The company sold this book at the following rates:

Retail (General Public)	$8.95
Libraries	$6.00
Wholesale	$4.50

   The company sold the following number of books by category:

Retail	5,000 copies
Libraries	2,500 copies
Wholesale	12,500 copies

   Identify each proof according to its classification of type: statistical, quotation, specific example, or illustration.

3. Using the information and setting outlined in exercise 2 above, create two separate non-artistic proofs of different types. Identify each as to the type of proof.

4. Complete the "Persuasive Speech Preparation Checklist" in Appendix F of this book on at least one speech assignment in this course.

5. Take the speech entitled "Widow: A Harsh and Hurtful Word" which is printed in Appendix D and make an analysis of the speaker's use of supporting material. Follow the format used in Figure 8.1 of this chapter.

Communicating on the Interpersonal Level*

*By Carley H. Dodd.

OBJECTIVES ✌

After completing this chapter, you should be able to:

1. *Understand* barriers to interpersonal communication.
2. *Communicate* more effectively with peers and others.
3. *Understand* the dynamics of successful interpersonal communication.
4. *Withstand* interpersonal conflict and work toward solutions of problems.
5. *Perform* more adequately in interviewing through a heightened awareness of interview dynamics.

As Chapter 1 indicated, interpersonal communication includes small group communication and dyadic communication. This chapter will focus upon interpersonal communication in the dyad, where two people engage in mutual verbal interaction. The goal of this chapter is to provide awareness of interpersonal communication dynamics and improve the practice of this important medium of exchange.

Understanding those dynamics first involves a process of self-awareness. Test yourself by taking the following Self-Report Interpersonal Communication Inventory. No one else is going to see the results, so be honest with yourself.

Self-Report Interpersonal Communication Inventory

Respond to each statement by marking strongly agree (SA), agree (A), neutral or undecided (U), disagree (D), or strongly disagree (SD).

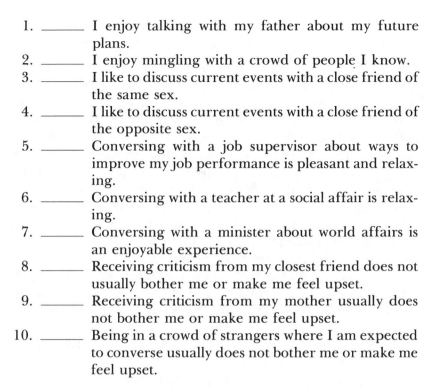

1. _____ I enjoy talking with my father about my future plans.
2. _____ I enjoy mingling with a crowd of people I know.
3. _____ I like to discuss current events with a close friend of the same sex.
4. _____ I like to discuss current events with a close friend of the opposite sex.
5. _____ Conversing with a job supervisor about ways to improve my job performance is pleasant and relaxing.
6. _____ Conversing with a teacher at a social affair is relaxing.
7. _____ Conversing with a minister about world affairs is an enjoyable experience.
8. _____ Receiving criticism from my closest friend does not usually bother me or make me feel upset.
9. _____ Receiving criticism from my mother usually does not bother me or make me feel upset.
10. _____ Being in a crowd of strangers where I am expected to converse usually does not bother me or make me feel upset.

Now that you have completed your response to each item, score each item by the following scale: SA = 5, A = 4, U = 3, D = 2, SD = 1. Finally, add all the scores so that you now have a total score for all the questions. (Incidentally, the interval reliability for this index is .78.)

How did you score? If you did not score over 30, this chapter can help you discover ways of becoming a more confident interpersonal communicator. Even if you scored high on the scale, you should benefit from this chapter. Understanding the dynamics of interpersonal communication should heighten one's sensitivity and assist him/her to become a better communicator. This chapter attempts to provide just such a foundation of awareness. Incidentally, you may want to take this same inventory after you have had a chance to digest the ideas discussed here and note any improvements.

Variables That Affect Interpersonal Communication

Any attempt to explain interpersonal communication relationships must include the factors that help produce the observed results: namely, communication with others. For example, some people feel nervous in talking with doctors, lawyers, professors, or bank presidents. In part, the cause of the anxiety may be related to the other person's higher status, his or her role, or perhaps the power we perceive the person to possess. By understanding the effects of role, status, and power you can more easily understand your behavior and others'. As you think of interpersonal communication, imagine viewing a beautiful building from different sides. No one side provides a complete view. Likewise, interpersonal communication has numerous dimensions. We can picture a multidimensional process with various intervening factors that help or hinder the effects of each communication situation. The model below illustrates:

MESSAGE → INTERVENING FACTORS → EFFECTS

Let us consider several intervening factors.

The Effects of Setting: Human Ecological Factors

The first consideration for effective interpersonal communication revolves around understanding the situation or setting. Most observers realize that temperature, size of the room, closeness (proximity) of furniture arrangement, and even color and styles of the immediate environment influence interpersonal communication. However, two features not as obvious as the environmental factors are what we might call *human ecological factors:* (1) the influence of the small group setting, and (2) the influence of the organizational setting upon interpersonal communication.

Small group networks (settings) influence interpersonal communication among members.[1] For instance, Figure 9.1

[1] See Marvin E. Shaw, *Group Dynamics*, 2nd ed. (New York: McGraw-Hill, 1976).

Wheel

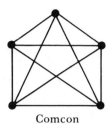

Comcon

Figure 9.1

shows two kinds of small group networks. As we saw in Chapter 1, when the network resembles the wheel (members cannot talk with others but only with the person in the middle), interpersonal communication is stifled. Research indicates that under such conditions, members feel individually alienated and quite dissatisfied with their interpersonal communication. The wheel reminds us of a classroom situation or a work crew and foreman when interpersonal communication occurs with the central person. By contrast, the comcon is an arrangement that allows all members to interact freely with each other. A network that encourages total interaction, like the comcon, results in the opportunity for greater clarity and fuller expression, necessary ingredients for effective interpersonal communication.

A second factor revolves around the influence of the *total organization and structure* upon interpersonal communication. Consider for a moment employer-employee problems in a business or industrial setting. One problem in such relationships, for instance, stems from differences in word meanings. In one study of language usage in an industrial setting, the research indicated that managers' connotative meanings differed from employee's meanings. Specifically, words that elicited highly different reactions fell into two different clusters: (1) words about traditional management objectives (incentives, quota, and budget), and (2) words common to modern management (communication, conferences, and cooperation).[2]

---

[2]A. K. Korman, "A Cause of Communications Failure," *Personnel Administration* 23 (1960): 17–21.

While semantics is a problem in any setting, *message distortion* is particularly germane to interpersonal communication within the organizational setting. Research reveals that people communicate with those geographically closest to them, such as members of a subgroup or department within a large organization. Although frequent interpersonal contact among subgroup members is good, some messages can be distorted. Spatial distance, for instance, may cause distortion because the subgroup members do not share the same frame of reference. Consequently, interpersonal communication between members of two different departments (horizontal communication) or between a departmental member and an executive (vertical communication) may suffer from message distortion. Figure 9.2 visually summarizes the problems in this type of human ecological setting.

In further exploring the effects of the organizational setting on interpersonal communication, we can describe other communication failures.

1. Although there is the illusion that expression is communication, merely speaking does not ensure its reception.
2. We fail to understand that listening is as important as speaking.
3. Messages supporting the "status quo" are received better than those concerning change.
4. Executives tend to overcommunicate orders and discourage upward communication that is not reinforcing.
5. Filtering of threatening or disquieting ideas occurs, especially in proportion to job security.
6. Executives fail to recognize that information going down the hierarchy usually moves rapidly, while upward information progresses slowly.
7. All levels of employees tend to look for formulas or gimmicks instead of trying to resolve deep problems.
8. An organization should not be perceived as a unit but as a series of pockets of people with multiple interpersonal communication links.[3]

[3]C. Goetziner and M. Valentine, "Problems in Executive Interpersonal Communication," *Personnel Administration* 27 (1964): 24–29.

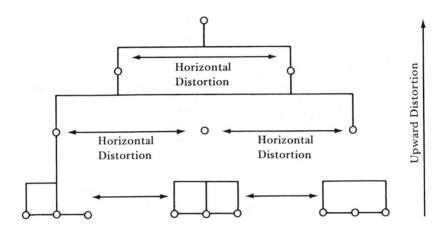

Interpersonal communication can fail between members of subgroups
or between managers communicating horizontally or between subgroup
members and an executive in upward communication.

Figure 9.2

Homophily: Similarity Between Communicators

A second intervening variable in the interpersonal communication process is the degree of similarity, or homophily, between
individuals engaged in an interpersonal interaction. Most of us
realize that we listen to our friends more than we listen to
strangers, but perhaps we never realized the subtle reasons.
You have probably had the experience of making a new ac-
quaintance and having your conversation go unusually well
from the beginning. These phenomena may be explained
partly by the variable we call *homophily.*

Homophily includes similarity in *appearance.* A person who
dresses like me is a person with whom I may feel more comfortable. Likewise, perceived similarity in *background* (age, education, ethnicity, residence, or geographical region), usually produces a more immediate sense of heightened interpersonal
communication. When two communicators share *attitudes and
values* on a moral or political question, for instance, they initially

find themselves on a deep level of interpersonal communication with a significant degree of satisfaction.[4] Even between members of two different cultures, research demonstrates that their interpersonal communication is far more effective when homophily exists. For instance, two researchers in Colombia found that informal interaction among traditional farmers occurred between farmers of similar background. When Colombian farmers discuss new farm ideas, they usually do not discuss the innovations with large landowners. Rather, lines of communication flow horizontally: small farmers converse with other small farmers.[5] The next time you converse with someone, ask yourself if this factor of homophily influences any of your conversation.

The Effects of Personality

Personality variables also affect the outcomes of interpersonal communication. Let us examine several of the most frequently occurring personality dynamics.

DOGMATISM   Have you ever wondered why sometimes you can talk until you are "blue in the face" and yet you seem unable to convince another person of some idea? While there may be numerous reasons you did not convince that person, one reason stems from the receiver's open and closed mindedness. The variable describing open and closed mindedness is *dogmatism*.[6] Highly dogmatic individuals are characterized by their highly rigid thought patterns, negative attitudes, and their low tolerance for inconsistency. Archie Bunker in "All in the Family"

[4]James C. McCroskey and Lawrence R. Wheeless, *Introduction to Human Communication* (Boston: Allyn and Bacon, 1976), pp. 109–13; See also James C. McCroskey, Virginia P. Richmond, and John A. Doly, "The Development of a Measure of Perceived Homophily in Interpersonal Communication," *Human Communication Research* 1 (1975): 323–32.

[5]Everett M. Rogers with Lynne Svenning, *Modernization Among Peasants: The Impact of Communication* (New York: Holt, Rinehart and Winston, 1969), pp. 234–35.

[6]Milton Rokeach, *The Open and Closed Mind* (New York: Basic Books, 1960).

illustrates the highly dogmatic personality. Archie, like many closed minded individuals, somewhat surprisingly is able to be persuaded by a highly authoritarian and credible source. Your awareness of this factor may help you understand better when it sometimes seems you are getting nowhere in your attempts to communicate with others.

Need for Acceptance   Nearly all of us have a need to be accepted by others. That need accounts for people joining various groups. However, some personality types need more acceptance than others. Sometimes an individual may talk incessantly, making mutual conversation difficult. While this person seems boring, he or she may be expressing a deeper need for acceptance. Likewise, the extremely quiet person may express a need for acceptance and a fear of rejection by his or her silence. Because of their needs, such personalities are motivated to maintain group loyalties.[7] Such individuals are probably susceptible to persuasion from others by whom they want to feel accepted, while they may resist counternorm communication (contrary to their value system) from sources irrelevant to the need for acceptance or fear of rejection.[8] Consequently, an overriding factor in certain interpersonal communication experiences stems from acceptance needs. Therefore, one's use of threatening messages or sarcasm can have a discouraging effect on other people. To establish and maintain rapport, use positive "bridge building" communication.

Copers and Avoiders   Have you ever noticed how some people seem able to stick with a point of discussion and solve problems, while other people avoid working toward solutions to problems? "Copers" are those individuals who generally work through problems, while "avoiders" are those individuals who usually either are unable or do not want to seek solutions to issues. Husbands or wives may choose to ignore problems and even flee various issues instead of maintaining an open line of

[7]Carl I. Hovland, Irving L. Janis, and Harold H. Kelley, *Communication and Persuasion* (New Haven: Yale University Press, 1953), p. 138.
[8]Herbert I. Abelson, *Persuasion* (New York: Springer Publishing, 1959), p. 28.

communication. Getting overwhelmingly angry, hiding behind a newspaper over the breakfast table, or giving the "silent treatment" are manifestations of avoiding behavior. Although the problem of avoidance may have deep-seated roots, concrete methods for coping with a question or issue between people exist. The following procedure may prove to be helpful:

1. Discuss the difficulty and define the area that seems to be the problem. Do not discuss the *other person,* only the issue and how the issue is showing itself.
2. Work toward laying out all possible *alternatives* that serve as solutions for the problem area. No matter how "crazy" the solution seems, consider it as an alternative. Since you are just "brainstorming" at this point, do not evaluate the solutions.
3. Work toward choosing *one solution.* Deciding on one may be a tedious task and each person may have to compromise. At this point, force yourself to keep an open mind. Do not revert to the temptation to attack the other person. Stick with objectively choosing the solution. If you do nothing more than agree or disagree, that may be a positive step toward future coping. If you just agree to keep the lines of communication open, that too is positive. At any rate, try to agree on some *action* to be taken. Remember to keep trying if your solutions do not work as you had planned.

Self-Concept

Self-concept refers to one's attitude about oneself. How you feel about yourself relates to how you communicate with another person. A person with a positive self-concept easily accepts others, withstands criticism, and copes with problems. In general a negative self-concept leads to pessimism, a feeling that "nobody likes me," sensitivity to criticism, and overresponsiveness to praise.[9]

[9]William D. Brooks and Philip Emmert, *Interpersonal Communication* (Dubuque, Iowa: William C. Brown Publishers, 1976), pp. 42–43.

For example, a person with a low self-concept might demonstrate extreme hypersensitivity at even the slightest hint of criticism, and yet complain frequently and criticize others. Positive communication genuinely emphasizing positive aspects of this person would very likely improve his or her self-concept. One's attitude toward self is probably the single most important contributor to success or failure in almost any life experience.

Source Credibility

Chapter 8 noted the importance of *ethos* or the impact of the source of communication on persuasion. Ethos, or source credibility, is also important for interpersonal communication. In general, when source credibility is high, a listener places more attention and importance on the communication and tends to be more easily persuaded. For example, suppose an employer is anticipating hiring someone whose credentials look highly promising on paper. Perhaps the prospective employee has experience, superb educational background, and outstanding recommendations. By credentials and reputation, therefore, this person's credibility is high. When the employer subsequently interviews this person, the previously established credibility may influence the employer in such a way that every aspect of the interview is perceived positively. In some ways, high source credibility is like a halo hanging over the communicator which causes us to perceive almost everything about that person positively.

Yet, source credibility is also a phenomenon developed and maintained throughout the course of the interpersonal relationship. Consider, for a moment, that same person with high credentials and reputation. Suppose during the job interview the person dressed sloppily, spoke with no enthusiasm, demonstrated a negative attitude toward other people, and showed no ability to answer questions about the prospective job. This person obviously would fail to receive the job. But why? Credibility hinges not only on person A's reputation, but credibility emerges from person B's perception of A. Person B, furthermore, perceives A in terms of five factors: (1) the *expertness* of the communicator; (2) the *trustworthiness* (perceived honesty, dependability) of the communicator; (3) the *sociability* or friendliness of the communicator; (4) *homophily* (co-orientation) between the communicator and his listener; and (5) the *dynamism* or enthusiasm of the speaker.[10]

Self-Disclosure

Self-disclosure refers to information that a person conveys about himself to another person. Research reveals a strong relationship between self-disclosure and trust. As interpersonal trust increases, self-disclosure increases. Furthermore, in the presence of sufficient self-disclosure, the chances are greater that a fondness for the other person will occur.[11] Of course, just telling about yourself indiscriminately does not necessarily produce positive effects, but a climate of self-disclosure can produce trust just as trust can produce self-disclosure. Unless two people share or disclose at some level, they remain strangers, dwarfed in a never growing relationship and seldom aware of the other's needs.

Researchers have reported differences in self-disclosure between males and females. The results of one recent study indicated that females tended toward more self-disclosure than males. Females demonstrated even greater self-disclosure toward persons they knew well. Also, females revealed more negative and honest information through less guarded control over the depth of the self-disclosure.[12] By contrast, perhaps

[10]Christopher J. S. Tuppen, "Dimensions of Communicator Credibility: An Oblique Solution," *Speech Monographs* 41 (1974): 253–60; David K. Berlo, James B. Lemert, and Robert J. Mertz, "Dimensions for Evaluating the Acceptability of Message Sources," *Public Opinion Quarterly* 33 (1969–70): 563–76.

[11]Brooks and Emmert, *Interpersonal Communication,* p. 209; See also Sydney Jourard, *The Transparent Self* (Princeton, N.J.: Van Nostrand Reinhold Co., 1964), pp. 25–27.

[12]Lawrence R. Wheeless and Janis Grotz, "Self-Disclosure and Trust: Conceptualization, Measurement, and Interrelationships" (A paper presented at the International Communication Association Convention, Chicago, April 1975).

males have unknowingly adopted a "strong and silent" image in their interpersonal communication. It should be stressed, however, that lines of communication must remain open for increased sharing and liking. Without such sharing, interpersonal communication is unlikely to advance beyond merely a superficial level.

Dominance-Submission Relationships

Animal studies reveal an interesting comparison with human behavior. For instance, Jane Goodall's study of chimps in East Africa demonstrates various modes of dominance and submission. Studies of birds, such as chickens, show that a "pecking order" of dominance and submission is established in a coop, where the birds literally peck one another to establish a hierarchy. After the order is established, the pecking becomes symbolic; one bird acts as if it is going to peck while the other bird bows in submission. Likewise, dogs lie on their backs and expose their throats to display symbolic submission.

Humans also display modes of dominance and submission in their verbal and nonverbal communication. How do you feel, for instance, when talking with a close personal friend? More than likely the dominance-submission variable is not operating. How do you feel when you visit a professor in his office? Perhaps you feel a bit more submissive. The same feeling is generally true in various relationships such as the employer-employee, officer–enlisted man, doctor-nurse, and parent-child relationships. When dominance and submission behavior is formalized, the relationship is called *superior-subordinate*.

Furthermore, certain dominant-submissive behavior can be explained by the roles people play. *Roles* are behaviors performed because of attitudes or expectations of position. A person may communicate and behave in a certain way because his or her role demands such behavior. A policeman who seems hard and unbending in his work role may be highly sympathetic and jovial with his family or friends. The clerk at a local department store who communicates cheerfully, demonstrating all measures of judiciousness and consideration for the potential customer, may be cruel and inconsiderate at home. Many of our interpersonal communication experiences may well be characterized by communication expected from the role rather than from the "real" person. *Power* relationships, in which one person has a perceived control over the other, and our perception of *status* of another person help explain relationships of dominance and submission.

Nonverbal Variables

Although people accept the adage "actions speak louder than words," few individuals know the reasons. Nonverbal communication within an interpersonal communication relationship mediates the relationship in such a way that sometimes nonverbal language completely overshadows the verbal. In fact, nonverbal language occurs in numerous ways but especially in two areas: proxemics and kinesics. (See also Chapter 1.)

PROXEMICS Proxemics refers to people's spatial relationships. Individuals unconsciously structure the space immediately surrounding the physical body. This space acts much like a personal boundary. Invasion of that boundary and its territory called *personal space* leads to responsive behavior. E. T. Hall noted that personal space is culturally determined and results from varying relationships. Hall further observed that space communicates and thus affects our interpersonal relationships:

> The flow and shift of distance between people as they interact with each other is part and parcel of the communication process. The normal conversational distance between strangers illustrates how important are the dynamics of space interaction. If a person gets too close, the reaction is instantaneous and automatic—the other person backs up. And if he gets too close again, back we go again. I have observed an American backing up the entire length of a long corridor while a foreigner whom he considers pushy tries to catch up with him. This scene has been enacted

thousands and thousands of times—one person trying to increase the distance in order to be at ease, while the other tries to decrease it for the same reason, neither one being aware of what was going on.[13]

Hall also indicated that voice shifts accompany specific ranges of distances:[14]

1. Very close (3 in. to 6 in.)   Soft whisper; top secret
2. Close (8 in. to 12 in.)   Audible whisper; very confidential
3. Near (12 in. to 20 in.)   Indoors, soft voice; outdoors, full voice; confidential
4. Neutral (20 in. to 36 in.)   Soft voice, low volume; personal subject matter
5. Neutral (4½ ft. to 5 ft.)   Full voice; information of nonpersonal matter
6. Public distance (5½ ft. to 8 ft.)   Full voice with slight over-loudness; public information for others to hear
7. Across the room (8 ft. to 20 ft.)   Loud voice; talking to a group
8. Stretching the limits of distance   20 to 24 ft. indoors; up to 100 ft. outdoors; hailing distance, departures

Research in proxemic behavior as a nonverbal communication variable reveals several patterns of interpersonal distance varying with race and sex. In one experimental study. Rosegrant and McCroskey discovered that (1) males establish greater interpersonal distance from males than they do from females, than females do from males, or than females do from females; (2) whites establish greater interpersonal distance from blacks than they do from whites, than blacks do from whites, or than blacks do from blacks; (3) female blacks establish closer dis-

[13]E. T. Hall, *The Silent Language* (New York: Doubleday, Anchor Books, 1973), p. 180.
[14]Ibid., pp. 184–85.

tances than female whites or either black or white males.[15] Friendship and trust are other factors which relate to closer spatial distances.

KINESICS   Kinesics refers to human body movement and its relation to communication. Certain kinds of body movements are physiological, such as yawning, stretching, or relaxing. Other kinesic patterns such as staring, walking slumped over, raising a clenched fist, and showing a victory sign are significant for communication. For instance, when you say "hello" to someone, probably you use a gesture for greeting such as the palm of your hand extended outward and upward in the manner we call "waving." The way we fold our arms, the direction of our body orientation (toward or away from the other person), the direction of our eye contact, and our manner of sitting and walking in the presence of others are significant nonverbal communication movements. Others can quickly decide if we are angry or pleased with them, just as we can read their body language. As you observe kinesics, note possible attitudes and the types of relationships (friends, strangers, and so forth). Perhaps you will want to practice positive nonverbal kinesic behaviors such as maintaining eye contact, controlling the use of gestures when speaking informally, guarding personal posture, and practicing facial features that convey warmth and friendliness.

The Dynamics of Dyadic Interpersonal Communication

We have all had the experience of feeling like something was not quite right in our interpersonal relationships. While some interpersonal conflicts heal with time, some only fester and become worse. Why does one experience interpersonal conflict? The answer can in part be explained by examining

[15]Teresa J. Rosegrant and James C. McCroskey, "The Effects of Race and Sex on Proxemic Behavior in an Interview Setting," *Southern Speech Communication Journal* 40 (Summer, 1975): 408–20.

balance theories of interpersonal communication. As you read these explanations, evaluate them in terms of your own interpersonal conflicts.

Balanced Relationships

Fritz Heider was an early social psychologist who examined the problem of interpersonal conflict. Heider observed how a given person, A, perceived different objects of reality or topics under discussion, X, and how he perceived another person, B.[16] In its extended form this notion of balanced relationships suggests that if you and another person like the same thing and like each other, a balanced relationship exists. However, an unbalanced relationship exists when people who like each other do not like the same things or when two people who like the same things do not like each other. (See Figure 9.3.)[17] The first component in this description of interpersonal relationships is A's orientation toward X, which includes his attitude toward X (approach

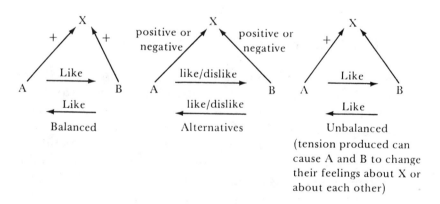

Figure 9.3   *Balanced and Unbalanced Relationships*

[16]Fritz Heider, *The Psychology of Interpersonal Relations* (New York: John Wiley and Sons, 1958). Heider's original notions were P-O-X instead of A-B-X proposed by Newcomb.

[17]Theodore Newcomb, "An Approach to the Study of Communicative Acts," *Psychological Review* 60 (1960): 393–404.

or avoidance) and various beliefs about X (cognitive attributes). The second component is A's orientation toward B. A and B can have positive or negative attractions as persons while holding favorable or unfavorable attitudes toward X. When there is an unbalanced state (A and B like each other but A feels positively about some topic X while B feels negatively about X), tension develops to restore balance through communication.

Several possibilities exist by which balance is restored. For example, suppose Bill (A) and Sally (B) like each other (they have been dating for one year). Bill likes sports cars (X) but Sally hates sports cars (X). In this obviously unbalanced situation (potentially producing some degree of conflict) several possibilities exist for change. To restore balance: (1) Bill may convince Sally to change her attitude toward sports cars (or Sally may convince Bill); (2) Bill may change his feelings about Sally or Sally about Bill; or (3) they may agree to tolerate the inconsistency. When you fail to convince someone, notice if your feelings toward that person change, even slightly. Understanding these concepts of balance can help us know how to prevent unpleasant feelings before they occur.

Cognitive Dissonance: Why We Rationalize After Decisions

Have you ever found yourself rationalizing your actions after you just bought something that you really could not afford? Or have you ever felt uncomfortable worrying about a statement that a highly respected person made to you when that statement contradicted one of your beliefs? The phenomenon of conflict after a decision or in the presence of information different from our beliefs is called *cognitive dissonance*. The theory suggests that two cognitive elements (or beliefs), A and B, are *consonant* when no inconsistency exists between them but *dissonant* when inconsistency exists.[18] For example, suppose you just read a scientific report which indicates the nutrient deficiency of a breakfast cereal you have used for three years because you thought it was nutritious. The resulting internal conflict is cognitive dissonance. Or, suppose you bought a car for $4,000 and

[18]Leon Festinger, *A Theory of Cognitive Dissonance* (Evanston, Ill.: Row, Peterson, 1957).

soon afterward learned that you could have bought the same car for only $3,500. Again, dissonance is aroused.

In the presence of dissonance people tend to rationalize in several predictable directions:

1. *Ignore the inconsistency.* In some cases, people will not only ignore the situation (hoping it will go away perhaps) but flee any situation in which conflict might arise, such as getting up and leaving an intolerable conversation.
2. *Discredit the source.* If someone's statement causes psychological discomfort, a person may simply think "he doesn't know what he is talking about" and thus reduce the inconsistency.
3. *Reduce the importance of the unchosen alternative.* In the car example, a person may convince himself that the dealer for the $3,500 car would not provide good service.
4. *Magnify the importance of the chosen alternative.* Not only can we minimize the importance of one cognitive element, but we can magnify the importance of the other. For instance, we might assume that the $4,000 car has numerous advantages over the $3,500 car, such as a preferred color and other minor features.
5. *Change attitude or behavior.* In some cases, we change our inconsistent attitudes and behaviors toward consistency. If one says he loves humankind but his actions indicate he hates the French, then he could stop hating the French or quit believing he loves humankind.

Numerous other examples exist, but many interpersonal and intrapersonal frustrations can be explained through a rudimentary awareness of these consistency theories.

A Practical Consideration of Interpersonal Communication: The How-to of Interviewing

Since interviewing is one type of interpersonal or dyadic communication process, let us now look at some practical suggestions about the interviewing process. In the interview, a face-to-face relationship is established through a direct interaction between the source and the receiver. The interview is unique in that its success depends on the success of the interaction between the two people and in that it provides a method that focuses on specific information. Let us outline several conditions of the interview for ready reference.[19]

DEFINITION OF INTERVIEW   Interviewing is a process of information-gathering that involves at least two persons. At least one of those persons has a definite purpose. In another sense, the interview is a bipolar type of communication, with direct interaction between the parties involved.

PURPOSES OF THE INTERVIEW   Communication researchers normally conceive of at least four basic purposes of interviews:

1. Dissemination of information (teacher-student interviews, news reports, feature stories).
2. Problem-solving and decision-making (employment interviews, appraisal, medical communication, counseling, grievance procedures, military debriefing, parent-teacher interaction).
3. Inducing belief and behavior (sales, prisoner-of-war interrogations, counseling, evaluation, disciplinary action).
4. Research and discovery of new information (casework, market research, police interrogation, author research, polls and opinion surveys).

CATEGORIES OF INTERVIEW INFORMATION   The message is obviously the chief factor in the interview. Messages within the interview can be classified according to the type of information they convey:

1. *Statements of description.* In this case, the interviewee provides an account of something he or she observed, much like a witness interrogated by a lawyer.

---

[19]See John Keltner, *Interpersonal Speech Communication: Elements and Structures* (Belmont, Ca.: Wadsworth Publishing Company, 1970); William D. Brooks, *Speech Communication* (Dubuque, Iowa: William C. Brown, 1971).

2. *Statements of factual knowledge.* This type of message is an explanation of information possessed. One example occurs when a university president calls a consultant for information.
3. *Statements of behavior.* The content of this message type defines the past, present, and future behavior of the respondent.
4. *Statements of attitude and belief.* These statements identify the respondent's foundation for judgment and commentary. They represent the respondent's evaluations (good-bad) and statements of truth or falseness about things.
5. *Statements of feelings.* These messages reveal physical and/or emotional levels reflecting the state of the individual. They indicate emotional states.
6. *Statements of value.* These statements convey long-abiding belief systems that are highly treasured by the respondent.

NONDIRECTIVE AND DIRECTIVE APPROACHES TO INTERVIEWING In a nondirective interview, the interviewer allows the respondent to steer the interview. The interviewer remains somewhat passive. In the directive interview, the interviewer dominates and controls the flow of information. The directive approach works best for discussion of specific items of information.

THE PROCESS OF QUESTIONING IN INTERVIEWING The quality of the questions in the interview determine its success or failure. There are several guides to good questioning:

1. The question must be fully understood by both parties.
2. Brief questions lead to more concise and qualitative answers. Long questions blend too many points simultaneously.
3. Suit the language of the question to the type of interview. Directive interviews demand explicit questions. Nondirective interviews demand more general questions.
4. Questions should not exceed the understanding level of the respondent.
5. For optimum progress only questions relevant to the subject matter should be asked.

6. A good question does not answer itself.
7. Avoid questions that require merely yes or no responses. Instead, utilize question words that encourage discussion, such as *what, why, how,* and *where.*
8. Throughout the questioning, continually observe the respondent's nonverbal behavior and adjust questions to the appropriate level of feedback.

COMMUNICATION CONDITIONS ESSENTIAL TO SUCCESSFUL INTERVIEWING   At least five communication conditions should be highlighted in the interviewer's concern for successful interviewing. The key phrases below anticipate those concerns:

1. *Familiar code.* Both participants must share a common set of words and jargon holding similar meaning for a set of words.
2. *Frame of reference.* Both parties in an interview should share a frame of reference including basic assumptions, expectations of the interview, the reasons for the interview, and its purpose. The interviewer may find it helpful to verbalize these features in the opening minutes of the interview.
3. *Freedom from ego threat.* Both parties should feel free from unfair treatment arising from statements made or from misunderstanding.
4. *Feedback.* Both persons should feed information back to the other to uncover errors in transmission or reception.
5. *Flow of information.* Repetition and restatement are essential to the fullest development of the interview. Therefore, both communicators should monitor and manage their rate of information exchange allowing a proper amount of time for "digestion of information."

Summary

This chapter examines interpersonal communication, focusing particularly on dyadic communication. The influence of intervening or mediating factors is also explored, including the influence of setting, homophily, personality variables, self-concept, source credibility, self-disclosure, dominance-submission, and nonverbal variables on dyadic communication. The chapter reports insights from balance theories applied to interpersonal communication and examines the phenomenon of cognitive dissonance. Finally, a practical guide to successful interviewing is supplied.

EXERCISES ౌ౪ఌ

1. Establish a role-playing situation with two people in your class.
    One person represents an irate customer and the other a
    lawnmower salesperson. The customer believes a new lawnmower
    was faulty and wants to return it after five hours of use for a full
    refund since the lawnmower quit running. The salesperson be-
    lieves the customer never put oil in the lawnmower. What do you
    observe in terms of roles? Nonverbal communication? Personality
    variables? Problem-solving?

2. Observe children at play. List mediating variables that you ob-
    serve in their communication and give examples. Report these
    findings to your class and exchange observations with other class
    members. How do children reflect and preshadow adult interper-
    sonal communication?

3. Do a field study where you observe dyads or pairs of people. Keep
    records. Notice nonverbal communication between friends and
    then compare with nonverbal communication between strangers.

4. Complete the Self-Report Interpersonal Communication Inven-
    tory on p. 168 again. How did your score compare with your
    earlier score in this chapter? List areas in which you want to
    challenge yourself to improve any aspect of your interpersonal
    communication.

Communicating in Groups*

✤ 10

*By J. Regis O'Connor.

OBJECTIVES ❧

After completing this chapter, you should be able to:

1. *Define* small group discussion and *describe* it in terms of its purposes and types.
2. *Identify* common formats for discussion, with examples.
3. Properly *word* a question for discussion.
4. *Prepare* and correctly *follow* a discussion outline.
5. *Identify* examples of cohesiveness, majority influence, role, and status as they surface in an actual discussion.
6. *Discuss* the major functions of discussion leadership.

If you hate war, you share the common hope that "discussing differences rather than fighting over them is the way of the future."[1] Discussing in groups is rapidly becoming the most widely used form of interpersonal communication in modern society. Whether it be at international peace talks, in a labor-management negotiating session, or in T groups, the popularity of group communication is on the rise. In the world of business, "According to various studies, managers spend up to 50 percent of their time in meetings."[2] The average citizen discusses the upcoming election with neighbors, the decision on busing with the school board, and the new zoning law with city

[1] Excerpt from Paul Harvey News, February 29, 1972.
[2] Roger A. Golde, "Are Your Meetings Like This One?" *Harvard Business Review*, I (1972): p. 68.

commissioners. *Group discussion occurs any time two*[3] *or more*[4] *persons orally cooperate to solve a common problem, arrive at a decision, or answer a question of mutual interest.*

The idea of "cooperation" is fundamental to discussion. It means that the discussants agree that they wish to achieve a common goal (even though they may not always wish to achieve that goal in exactly the same ways). Cooperation means that each member of the group primarily devotes his energies to achieving a solid group outcome (rather than promoting *his* pet solution or opinions).[5] This does not say that there won't be differences of opinion in a discussion group—only that each member should enter the group with an open mind, genuinely prepared to listen as well as to argue.

The idea that discussion groups form for a definite purpose is also important. Simple talk or conversation is not group discussion. Ordinarily, each discussion takes place only when you come *prepared*, in much the same way that you would prepare if asked to give a public speech. Groups form to achieve definite and sometimes urgent goals. If you have not prepared actively to participate and achieve those goals, you are dead weight in the group. However, if you have researched well, you can have considerable influence in forming the group's decision.

Types of Group Discussion

Discussion groups fall into a number of different types. We all realize there are differences (other than the topic being dis-

[3]Usually interaction between just two persons is thought of as some form of dyadic communication, such as an interview or a conversation. However, for a discussion of two as sufficient to constitute a group, see John W. Keltner, *Interpersonal Speech Communication: Elements and Structures* (Belmont, Ca.: Wadsworth Publishing Company, 1970), p. 291.

[4]Ernest G. Bormann claims the optimum size for a discussion group is from five to seven; *Discussion and Group Methods: Theory and Practice* (New York, Harper & Row, Publishers, 1969), pp. 3–4.

[5]For a detailed treatment of the effectiveness of cooperation in groups, see Morton Deutsch, "The Effects of Cooperation and Competition upon Group Process," in Dorwin Cartwright and Alvin Zander, *Group Dynamics: Research and Theory*, 3rd ed. (New York: Harper & Row, 1968), pp. 461 ff.

cussed) between a meeting of the board of directors of General Motors Corporation and a group of NBC commentators discussing the Mideast War on the *Today* show. The board of directors has no listening audience—the commentators are speaking to hundreds of thousands of television viewers. The board of directors has the power to put its policies into action—the commentators can only suggest (or at most, recommend) solutions for the social problems they discuss. The board of directors is probably gathered mainly to decide policy rather than to instruct or teach—the commentators often wish to enlighten the television viewer.

If we divide discussion into types based on the *purpose* for the group's existence, we find that one of two reasons usually calls a group together—*decision-making* or *enlightenment*. The board of directors mentioned above probably has not come together mainly to learn how the corporation is growing (although they might spend some time reporting its status). Primarily they are gathered to decide upon *action* for the future. The TV commentators, on the other hand, may be personally concerned about the war in the Mideast, but their primary purpose in discussing it with nationwide coverage is to make the listeners more aware.

The second major way in which discussion groups differ from one another depends on who is mentally present to the discussants while the discussion is in progress. If the discussants are communicating only for the benefit of each other, the discussion is *closed-group*; if they communicate to listeners outside the discussion group (even though these may not be physically present, as in the case of a TV audience) it is *public* discussion.

Naturally, these various types of discussion can occur in combination. An open meeting of the board of directors, with all company employees present, would be an example of public enlightenment discussion. If the board invited employee participation in determining policy, it would then be public decision-making discussion. When a group of students gets together for group study before a big exam, it is closed-group enlightenment discussion. If those same students were gathered to plan a fraternity dance, the format would be closed-group decision-making.

Formats for Discussion

Probably the most common *format* for closed-group decision-making discussion is the *committee*—a small subgroup of a larger parent organization given a specific task or set of tasks to perform. Some committees have only the power to recommend action or policy to the larger body of which they are a part. Others can actually render a decision or carry out a task. A board of directors for a corporation is a special kind of elected committee, given the authority to carry out decision-making tasks for the entire membership.

A common format for closed-group enlightenment discussion is the *round table* discussion. Although this term is often used rather loosely to apply to almost any type of closed-group discussion, it most often means a closed-group session in which information-sharing or enlightenment of the participants is the object. A ladies' sewing club or a group of college English instructors discussing ways of improving classroom teaching would be using a round table format.

Public discussion often takes the form of a *panel*. In this format a group of experts on the topic under consideration discusses in front of a live or a media audience. The panel's purpose could be either enlightenment or decision-making, but in either case they are discussing for the benefit of an audience as well for themselves.

A similar format for public decision-making is the *symposium*. Only the pattern of communication distinguishes it from the panel. In a symposium, each expects to give a short, uninterrupted speech, followed by the next panel member and so on until all have spoken. A symposium is really a series of public speeches by experts and is thus not true group discussion since complete free interaction does not exist.

Either the panel or symposium can be opened up to questions or comments from the audience. When this is done, the format is called either a *panel-forum* or a *symposium-forum*. This arrangement can be quite effective both with a live audience or with media audiences where listeners or viewers can call in questions or reactions over the telephone.

Preparing for Discussion

The discussions that you hold in this class will not be entirely real life discussions. They will occur because your instructor assigns them, and their purpose will be to teach you group discussion method. This does not mean that you cannot *make* them real, however. They can apply to your interests, and to issues that are important to you. There is no reason a classroom group discussing an abortion bill pending in the state legislature shouldn't report its decision in a persuasive letter to the lawmakers, for instance.

Choosing the Topic

The first step in making a discussion a success is to choose the right topic. Your instructor will undoubtedly have a method for helping you with this but it should be a topic that has "interest, significance, and manageability."[6]

A well-chosen topic will be of interest to several persons or groups. If the format is one of public discussion, it should deal with a subject that the audience either is interested in already, or can become concerned about. The discussants themselves will naturally participate most effectively when the topic is of interest to the group and to each individual member.

It is not enough, however, that the topic be interesting. It should also be significant; that is, it should "materially affect the lives of the discussants (and the audience, if one is present) at

[6]David Potter and Martin Andersen, *Discussion: A Guide to Effective Practice*, 2nd ed. (Belmont, Ca.: Wadsworth Publishing Co., 1970), p. 4.

the time of the discussion."[7] For example, it might be interesting, but not significant, for a college-age group to discuss the question, "How can problems of adolescent immaturity best be handled?" The participants have probably solved most of their personal problems in this area and are still too young to be parents of teenage children. Of course, if most of the discussants were about to begin teaching in high school, such a topic might then become interesting and significant.

Finally, a well-chosen topic will be manageable. Discussion is a slow process at best, so you should not attempt to discuss the beliefs of the world's major religions in one hour. Choose a topic that you can reasonably hope to complete in the time allotted. If the time for research is limited, the topic will often need to be narrowed, or the research responsibilities divided among the group members during a prediscussion meeting.

Wording the Question

Almost as soon as a topic is chosen, someone needs to reduce the topic to a clear, concise, unbiased question.[8] Many discussions become cloudy, and many more fail to achieve productive results, because no one has taken the time to state carefully the question in a precise way. Precious minutes and sometimes even hours can be wasted in discussing a topic before someone in the group says, "But, wait a minute, I thought we were discussing only the *military* reasons for the U.S. involvement in the Mideast. Now we're on the political background. Just what is the question?"

For a question to lead to productive discussion, it should be *worded as a question* not as a statement. Furthermore, it should usually be a question that has more than two possible answers. A question like "Should free campus parking stickers be given to students?" allows only a "yes" or "no" answer. This tends to turn the discussion into a debate, with two group factions, each

[7]Ibid., p. 109. Parenthesis mine.

[8]See Halbert E. Gulley, *Discussion, Conference and Group Process,* 2nd ed. (New York: Holt, Rinehart and Winston, Inc., 1968), pp. 67–68 for a clear summary of rules for properly wording discussion questions.

arguing for its own opinion. A better way to phrase this question would be: "How should the problem of student parking be handled by the university?" With the question phrased in this manner, the use of free stickers becomes just one of several possible solutions for the discussion group to consider.

A well-worded question will also be *clear* and unambiguous. Vague questions, like "What about the campus parking problem?" should be avoided as should those with abstract words in key positions, such as "Is the Democratic Party's present platform progressive?" Each group member will probably understand "progressive" a little differently from every other member.

Conciseness is another virtue in a properly worded discussion question. Extremely long and involved wording can confuse rather than clarify a group session. Picture yourself trying to discuss the following wordy question: "When, and under what circumstances, should the administrative body of a university, with legal and moral consideration being taken into account, allow a student, nonstudent and other outside speakers to make use of university facilities (and sometimes sponsorship) for speaking engagements on topics of interest to both students and faculty?" Obviously, this somewhat exaggerated example could better be discussed with the wording: "What kinds of speaker policies should be established at our universities?" Most of the dependent ideas contained in the first example would be more properly included in the discussion outline than in the question.

Finally, if you are given the responsibility of wording a discussion question, be sure that your wording is *unbiased*. If you were a male chauvinist, for example, you would display your bias if you worded a question dealing with employment opportunities for women: "Is it *possible* for women to hold positions of major executive responsibility in industry?"

Types of Questions

Groups usually discuss one of three types of questions: questions of fact, questions of value, or questions of policy. Questions of *fact* deal with whether a situation exists, under what circumstances it exists, or how it may be defined. "Are we in an energy crisis?" is basically a question of fact, although it obviously involves a degree of interpretation of the word *crisis*. Groups do not discuss questions of scientific fact that could better be answered by research. A question like "What is the current rediscount rate paid by member banks to the Federal Reserve?" could be answered more efficiently by a single researcher than by a group.

Questions of *value* go a step beyond those of fact. While questions of fact deal with the existence of something, questions of value revolve around the worth of the object, person, or situation. If the discussion question primarily emphasizes whether a thing is good or bad, desirable or undesirable, promising or hopeless, or similar factors requiring judgments of worth, it is usually called a question of value. "Is the two-party system the best political system for the United States?" is an example of a question of value.

Questions of *policy* are usually the most complex type of discussion questions but are also those most commonly discussed. Questions like "What should be the university's policy regarding open visitation in dorms?" and "What role should the federal government assume in the fight against industrial pollution of our waterways?" are questions of policy. These often include the word *should,* and are directed toward some course of physical or mental action. Naturally, a group does not necessarily need to have the power to put their decision into action to discuss such a question. Many groups possess only recommendatory power, yet their influence remains considerable.

Preparing the Outline

If you were driving from New York to California for the first time, you would undoubtedly take a road map with you. You would probably plot the best route beforehand, and decide about how far you would drive each day. If you were on vacation, you wouldn't want to adhere strictly to a pre-set schedule, however. When an interesting looking side-trip presented itself along the way, you might take a half day's trip off your planned route to explore. A discussion outline serves much the same purpose as a vacation road map. It provides the necessary guidance to keep the group moving towards its goal, but it should never be adhered to so rigidly that it stifles spontaneity or creativity among the members. "Just as an extemporaneous speaker may modify his speech, so the discussion group can depart from their outline because of changing conditions."[9]

A policy question will often demand an outline having three main divisions or phases:

1. Analysis of the background and causes of the problem, or situation (orientation phase).
2. Consideration, evaluation, and comparison of various possible solutions (evaluation stage).
3. Agreeing and disagreeing about the best solution or decision (control phase).[10]

Most policy discussions would include each of these phases, usually outlined in the above order. The actual discussion, however, may sometimes move briefly into one of the latter phases before an earlier one is completed.

If the discussion question is one of fact rather than policy, ordinarily only phase 1 will be outlined and discussed. When the question is one of value, usually phases 1 and 2 are treated.

The kind of discussion outlines referred to above would ordinarily be drawn up by the entire group in a prediscussion meeting. They are general in nature and follow the format used for speech outlining (except that questions rather than statements are used in main heads and subheads). Before the actual discussion, the designated leader (or moderator) should draw up a more specific outline consisting of questions within

[9]Bormann, *Discussion and Group Methods*, p. 51.

[10]For a fuller treatment of the social and task-related variables characteristic of each phase, see Robert F. Bales and Fred L. Strodtbeck, "Phases in Group Problem Solving," *Journal of Abnormal and Social Psychology* XLVI (1951): 485–95.

each phase which he will use to stimulate group members' thinking during the discussion. It is probably desirable that this leader's outline not be distributed to the members in advance so that spontaneous answers will occur in the discussion. However, in some forms of public discussion, such as televised programs, it may be necessary to give the participants a preview of the kinds of questions that they will hear when on camera.

Selecting the Leadership

Three or four leadership formats are used in discussion, depending on such factors as the personalities of the group members, the purpose that has brought the group together and the size of the membership. It may be that a single individual will be appointed to fulfill all the functions of leadership; several group members may be asked to exercise different functions; or no assignment of functions may be made beforehand, in which case members would spontaneously step into leadership roles as the need would arise during the discussion. In any case, the discussion will run more smoothly when the leadership format to be used is decided beforehand by the members. This can often be accomplished in a prediscussion meeting.[11]

Group Interaction

Several interesting patterns begin to appear whenever people get together in groups. Five or ten mouths and minds dealing with a topic inevitably leads to a certain amount of confusion. As a discussant, or discussion leader, you can greatly reduce the amount of confusion if you understand group interaction and know what to expect.

[11]The various leadership formats are treated more fully beginning on p. 204.

Cohesiveness

People join groups not only to help the group achieve a goal, but for personal satisfaction as well. Both these ends are best achieved when the group has attained a high degree of cohesiveness. This means the kind of group loyalty that is reflected in the motto of the Commonwealth of Kentucky: "United we stand, divided we fall." Each member draws strength from the group unity, and the group unity is strengthened by the loyalty of the members. Groups whose cohesiveness is high tend to have livelier meetings than do groups with poor cohesiveness—more questions are asked, members are less bored, people feel more free to disagree and the group decision is important to the discussants. Groups with low cohesiveness have polite, but boring, meetings. Members want the meeting to end as quickly as possible, and even important decisions are made quickly with little or no disagreement or weighing of evidence.[12]

Majority Influence

A second factor of group influence is the natural tendency of groups to force conformity to the views of the majority. The outcome of a discussion question of policy ordinarily takes one of three forms: (1) *consensus,* which is unanimous agreement among all discussants; (2) *compromise,* in which each of two or more parties gives up part of its viewpoint and retains part; or (3) *majority vote* in which the majority decision becomes the decision of the entire group. Consensus is the most desirable outcome, since it means that all the group members are thoroughly committed to carrying out the group's decision. However, consensus that results from incomplete testing of opinions, or from one or more of the members' capitulating simply out of a desire to "go along with the majority" is worse than taking a vote. Groups must be very cautious about assum-

[12]For an excellent description of group cohesiveness, see Ernest G. Bormann and Nancy C. Bormann, *Effective Small Group Communication* (Minneapolis: Burgess Publishing Co., 1972), pp. 10–11.

ing that a timid member, who doesn't say much, is giving consent to the majority view by his silence. Too many silent members may mean that there is a considerable pocket of unspoken disagreement in the group. The leader and other group members should make every effort to tap all possible sources of honest opinion existing in the group.

Role and Status

Two more factors of psychological interaction are the concepts of *role* and *status*. Whenever persons remain in a particular group for even a brief period of time, each member begins to assume a particular role in the group. In group discussion terminology *role* means *the particular mixture of behaviors and communications that a member engages in, and is expected to engage in while a part of the group.* One member might come to be viewed as the group clown, or tension releaser, for example; another might assume the role of task leader—always pushing to have the group arrive at its decision; a third, the socializer—often getting the group off the subject into fascinating side issues.[13] Usually it takes some time for roles to stabilize within groups. A set of total strangers meeting for the first time for thirty minutes will probably begin the process of role emergence, but roles will not begin to emerge in any clearcut way during that brief time.[14]

When roles have been recognized and each group member feels satisfied with the role he finds himself in, the group grows much more cohesive and ready to tackle the task at hand efficiently.

Status means *the importance attached to each role by the group members.* In discussion groups, the role of leader is usually viewed as a high-status role. Other roles are accorded varying degrees of respect and reward, depending on how high or how low they are on the group's mental status ladder. Since high

[13]Bormann, *Discussion and Group Methods,* has a thorough discussion of the concept of role in the small groups, pp. 184–86.

[14]See Ernest G. Bormann, "The Paradox and Promise of Small Group Research," *Speech Monographs* XXXVII (1970): 211.

status positions carry with them rewards such as ego-gratification and esteem, they are eagerly sought by many group members. This competition can often lead to social pressures and tensions in the group's structure that may get in the way of efficient achievement of the task at hand. Members need to be aware that this kind of struggle is common in groups, and not allow it to completely overshadow accomplishment of the group goals.

Discussion Leadership

From the instant most groups are formed, certain members begin to exercise greater degrees of influence than do others. Such influence is referred to as group leadership. Early discussion researchers felt that leadership ability was something that was "in" certain persons and "not in" others—in other words, you either had it or you didn't. If you had it, you turned out to be the group leader; if you didn't, you would only be a follower, in practically any group you found yourself in. The more recent view is not quite so simple. It holds that a given group possesses a kind of group personality (called *syntality*)[15] analogous to an individual's personality. Whenever any group member says or does something that "has a demonstrable influence upon group syntality,"[16] he is exercising leadership in the group. If George makes a statement in the group meeting today that opens up an entirely new approach to the group's problem he is exercising leadership. Yesterday, under different circumstances, the group might have paid little or no attention to the comment. If so, George would not have been exercising leadership yesterday had he made the comment then.

All this is not to say that there aren't certain standard moves that group members make that are usually viewed as leadership moves. Like a public speech, a discussion may be

[15]cf. Raymond B. Catell, "New Concepts for Measuring Leadership in Terms of Group Syntality," *Human Relations* IV (1951): 161–84.
[16]Ibid., p. 175.

viewed as composed of three basic parts—a beginning, a middle, and an end. Whenever any group member fulfills one of the functions of beginning the discussion, regulating communication, or concluding, he will almost inevitably be functioning as a leader at that particular moment.

Beginning the Discussion

Naturally someone has to start the ball rolling in any discussion group. This includes: (1) introducing the topic to be discussed, either to the group or to the listening audience if the discussion is public; (2) providing sufficient background about the question to show why the group has assembled to discuss it; and (3) introducing the group members to each other and/or to the audience.

Regulating Communication

Several leadership functions must be attended to during the central part of any discussion: (1) making each member feel at ease to speak his or her mind fully and frankly—this means that the leader must not only invite, but encourage, members to contribute to the discussion, and promote the idea that each individual's ideas are valuable and need to be aired; (2) keeping participation balanced—naturally some members are going to talk more than others in any group. The leader needs to suppress tactfully those who tend to monopolize and gently draw in those who tend to be wallflowers; (3) suppressing fights—when two or more members begin debating (especially if the debate starts to deal in personal attacks) the leader has the unwelcome but necessary task of reminding the protagonists that discussion is a cooperative enterprise rather than a competitive one; (4) keeping the discussion on the track—this generally means recognizing major tangents from the prepared outline and inserting a gentle reminder to the group that it has gotten off onto a side issue. An excellent way for the leader to keep the discussion moving towards its goal is by making brief transitional summaries for the group after they complete discussion of a major segment of the outline; (5) clarifying—some group members often have excellent ideas, but aren't very successful at expressing those ideas clearly to the group. When this happens, it becomes the leader's job to save a potentially creative idea by saying something like "I think that's a fine idea, Sally! If I understand you correctly, you're saying . . ." then restating the idea in clearer terms so the other group members will understand it; and (6) watching the time limit—this can be an especially important leadership function in public discussions, such as those produced for radio or television.

Concluding

When the leader feels that the group has adequately covered the discussion question, or a pre-set time limit has almost been reached, he should: (1) summarize the major ideas and outcomes of the discussion, being careful not to overload the summary with *his* ideas; and (2) save enough time for each group member to disagree with the summary or insert a minority opinion.

In some discussion groups all of the above functions are taken care of by a single group member. Maybe he is the chairman of the board and all the leadership functions naturally fall to him. Or perhaps he is a member of a classroom discussion group and the other group members have elected him leader before the discussion takes place (or the teacher has appointed him leader). If, for whatever reason, all these functions fall to a single individual, he is called an *appointed leader*, and he ordinarily finds himself a very busy fellow during the discussion.

Some discussion experts suggest parcelling out the functions among several, or even among all of the group members—let one introduce, another keep participation balanced, another make transitions, a fourth tone down debates that arise, and so on. Still other researchers feel it is best not to appoint or assign any particular functions to anyone.[17] Ideally, all the group participants should understand leadership functions. If they do, one or another group member will handle each function of leadership as the need for it arises during discussion. This spontaneous form of leadership is known as *emergent leadership.*

Summary

Group communication is rapidly becoming one of the most widely used forms of social interaction. It occurs any time two or more persons orally cooperate to solve a common problem, arrive at a decision, or answer a question of mutual interest. Groups ordinarily form to enlighten each other (and the listeners, if present), or to arrive at a decision. Either of these basic purposes may be achieved with just the discussants themselves present (closed-group), or with an audience taken into account (public).

Effective discussion requires thorough preparation. This begins with choosing a topic that is interesting, significant, and manageable. The question must be carefully worded in such a way that it is open to alternative answers, is clear, concise, and unbiased. Next, an outline should be drawn up to serve as a general road map for the discussion without becoming so detailed as to render the discussion sterile and without spontaneity. Finally, the leadership format to be used should be decided upon. Commonly used formats are: (1) a single appointed leader; (2) several appointed leaders, each fulfilling designated functions; and (3) emergent leadership.

Knowledge of several factors of group interaction is important to understand group discussion. *Cohesiveness* is one such

[17]For a thorough discussion of various factors relating to leadership distribution, see Dorwin Cartwright and Alvin Zander, "Leadership and Performance of Group Functions: Introduction," in Cartwright and Zander, *Group Dynamics,* pp. 310–17.

factor—a group spirit that not only increases group productivity, but also augments the personal satisfaction of group members. *Majority opinion* is another factor of group interaction that often dictates which of the three basic outcomes a discussion session will produce—consensus, compromise, or majority vote. Finally, the operation of *roles* and *status* can frequently dictate whether a group meeting is productive and satisfying to the members, or inefficient and ego-punishing.

The most recent approaches to discussion leadership suggest that it be viewed in terms of the fulfilling of certain group functions (the influencing of group syntality). Generally the commonly recognizable functions fall into three categories: beginning the discussion; regulating communication, and concluding.

EXERCISES ✌

1. Divide the class into subgroups of five or seven members. a) Each member should come prepared to suggest a discussion topic (worded as a question) for later discussion by the group. b) The subgroup should decide which topic they will use for their later discussion.

2. These exercises all deal with a single discussion topic. They may be used individually or in the sequence listed.

   a. As a class, word a discussion question of policy, dealing with the parking problem on your campus. Check your wording against each of the five rules for properly wording a discussion question listed in the chapter.

   b. Divide the class into discussion groups of five or seven members each. Have each group hold a prediscussion meeting in which it prepares a discussion outline on the parking question, and decides on the leadership format for its group.

   c. All groups hold separate discussions simultaneously on the parking problem. By the end of one full class period, each group should have a solution ready to present to the entire class.

   d. Have the individual group leaders present their group's solution to the entire class. The class should then decide which is the best solution. (If voting must be used, no class member may vote for his or her own group's solution.)

   e. Have the instructor send a memorandum to the appropriate school official recommending that the class solution to the campus parking problem be considered.

Appendix A:
Model Student Speeches

A Heap Of Trouble[1]

What I am about to tell you, is a bunch of garbage. "In the beginning Man created the plastic bag and the tin and aluminum can and the cellophane wrapper and the paper plate and the disposable bottle and Man said this was good because Man could then take his automobile and buy all his food in one place and Man could save that which was good to eat in the refrigerator and throw away that which had no further use. And soon the earth was covered with plastic bags and tin and aluminum cans and paper plates and disposable bottles and there was no where to sit down or walk and Man shook his head and cried, 'look at this awful mess.'" These words written by Art Buchwald in 1970 are not as humorous today as they were a few years ago.

Ever since Eve ate the first apple, man has been plagued with the problem of what to do with the core. For a while sweeping it under the rug seemed to be the answer but soon the rug became lumpy and smelly. Then we thought maybe we could wash it down the sink but soon the sink became clogged. And when there was not a rug or a sink handy we just threw it along side of the highway.

Now it seems like everywhere we look there is garbage and it just keeps on coming. Fifty years ago the average American threw away every day a little over two and half pounds of garbage. Today each of us will create six pounds of trash, and it is projected by the Environmental Protection Agency by 1980

[1]Carl Hall, "A Heap of Trouble." Speech given at Interstate Oratorical Association at Peoria, Illinois, May 2–3, 1975.

considering all of our waste, our country will have to dispose of fifty pounds of refuse per person per day.

That sounds like quite a mess, doesn't it, but wait until you start adding your mess and my mess together. Last year we as a nation threw away one hundred and thirty million tons of garbage. This is enough trash to fill enough garbage trucks lined bumper-to-bumper to stretch from New York to Los Angeles, three abreast.

When I read that statement I asked the same question you are probably asking yourself right now. Where did we put all of it? Our city dump gobbled up over 84 percent of it but most all of our dumps have stopped gobbling and have started to nibble. It is projected that in the next five years half of America's dumps will have reached their capacity. The other 16 percent of last year's was either dumped in our water ways or scattered along our highways.

A survey was taken of a typical one mile stretch of two lane highways in Kansas. The collection revealed 770 paper cups, 730 empty cigarette packs, 590 beer cans, 130 soft drink bottles, 120 beer bottles, 110 whiskey bottles, and 90 beer cartons. But we don't have to go to Kansas to witness the failure of our one billion dollar a year "Keep America Beautiful" campaign.

Why has this campaign failed and why is garbage becoming the problem it is today? The answer to this question can be traced back in history to every affluent civilization since the world began . . . WASTEFULNESS. Today we are treating our world as though we have a spare in the trunk.

Every year Americans throw away eight million television sets, a large portion of which were in working order or in need of inexpensive repairs. Because we now can afford newer models seven million automobiles are junked each year, and because we don't want to be bothered with returnable containers, in the last decade our production of disposable bottles and cans has doubled, and if the present rate continues, in two years the only place we'll be able to find a returnable container will be in a museum.

It is this wasteful attitude that has made garbage collection the 5th largest industry and made garbage our nation's grossest national product. This year we Americans will spend four and a half billion dollars for refuse collection. This sum is exceeded only by our expenditures for schools, roads, and national defense. Our wastefulness is costing us dearly. If you live in Philadelphia it costs you forty million dollars a year. If you're from New York City the price is one hundred and fifty million dollars a year. For every newspaper copy the *New York Times* puts out it costs the city a dime to dispose of it and each edition one hundred and fifty acres of forest. New York's former Environmental Protection Administrator, Merrll Eisenbud, warns that the city could become buried under the seven million tons of refuse that it now generates annually if something drastic is not done quickly. During the garbage strike of 1968, New York was literally digging out from under 100,000 tons of trash after only a few days.

The 1970 strike by sanitation workers in the nation's capital shut down the District of Columbia's four incinerators and dirtied the city's streets and alleyways with appalling speed.

Dozens of other walkouts by underpaid municipal trash collectors in other communities have brought right to the doorsteps of millions of Americans the cold hard fact that waste management is a terribly serious daily concern.

The question then arises: will we wait to deal with this great social problem until it reaches the crisis stage as we did with our nation's energy situation or can you and I realize the urgency of our condition. The answer will be left up to us.

There is an answer to our impending crisis if we will commit ourselves to it. Conservation and utilization are the keys that can keep the lid on our nation's garbage can locked, and the garbage inside.

Recycling is a term that is familiar to all of us, but few have realized its great value. Maybe Senator Edmund Muskie, chairman of the pollution subcommittee of the Senate Committee on Public works, caught a glimpse of its importance when he said "if future generations of Americans are to inherit adequate economical supplies of our natural resources, we must move now to find new ways of reusing solid waste in this country." Former Secretary of the Interior, Stewart Udall, posed a probing question when he asked: "Why do we continue to dip into our natural resource reserves when we might be turning our choking wastes into wealth?" But what is this wealth Secretary Udall was talking about? Beer and soft drinks in returnable, reusable bottles cost less than the same beverages in disposable containers and reusable containers can be used as many as twenty times. Dr. Douglas Bynum, a research professor at Texas A & M has developed a technique for building better and cheaper roads by using ground-up glass, plastic containers, and rubber tires. In addition to ridding our country of seventy-five million discarded tires annually this method would cut road-building costs by as much as one-fifth. To help eliminate the seventy million automobiles we discard each year they can be shredded and used in concrete building blocks. But perhaps the most promising use of trash is its conversion into energy which could enable us to kill two birds with one rotten apple. In cities such as St. Louis and Baltimore experimental conversion plants are already in use converting garbage to electricity with satisfactory results.

With further development the potential is unlimited. Figures revealed in May of this year showed that within the one hundred and thirty million tons of garbage we threw away last year, there was enough unused energy to light the nation for a year.

. . . and then Man wiped his tears, rolled up his sleeves, and picked up the plastic bags, the tin and aluminum cans, the paper plates and disposable bottles and used them over again and again in as many ways as he could think of. Slowly, the earth began to be uncluttered, and Man said, "It is better."

Our world is already in a heap of trouble but let's not end up in a heap of trash.

Amnesty[2]

Saigon, April 29, 1975

All Americans evacuated. Government agrees to unconditional surrender. Quietly Americans at home watched the final episode of fourteen years of U.S. involvement in Southeast

[2]Roger Woodruff, "Amnesty." Speech given at Interstate Oratorical Association at Peoria, Illinois, May 2–3, 1975.

Asia. No longer do we care to blame anyone, be they U.S. presidents or political leaders, South Viet Nam's ex-political leaders, our fighting force, or even the South Vietnamese army who fled and in so doing killed and ravaged their own people. But rather today we have begun to focus our attention to the humanitarian needs of those involved in the situation. Presently we are trying to find homes for the more than 50,000 Viet Nam refugees. In the aftermath of the collapse of South Viet Nam we have offered them our homeland.

What of the American victims? The 140,000 young Americans refused amnesty and exiled from their country. Where shall be their homeland? The problem indeed is for Americans to solve. The problems, the lack of humanitarian concern for a generation of young Americans who several years ago brought our attention to the futility of this war by their refusal to participate, as the U.S. today has refused to participate any longer. The war, popular at first, not understood, then unpopular, and finally a complete misfortune for all concerned. Today, I ask you all to consider the plight of the American exile.

Four months ago, former Senator Charles Goodell, chairman of President Ford's amnesty board, requested of the President a six-month extension to the January 31, 1975 deadline for conditional amnesty. President Ford responded by granting an extension of twenty-eight days. And then once again three weeks later, based upon Mr. Goodell's request, the President signed the final extension to an already failing program. And on April 1, conditional amnesty expired, leaving us with a program of failure and a policy of no amnesty at all, which is certainly not a solution to the problem.

Now Mr. Goodell had predicated his arguments for these extensions based upon the fact that after all the program had seen a rather moderate amount of success. In fact, in its waning weeks there had been a rather high level degree of success in response to the program. And yet this is in clear contrast to the facts of the case. The facts are [that] of some 150,000 young men eligible for conditional amnesty only 5 percent responded by returning to the United States. This does seem to indicate that perhaps there was a problem with conditional amnesty.

The Amnesty Exile Association, whose membership is comprised of various members of amnesty organizations throughout the world, put forth in a joint policy statement what they considered to be the major overriding issues and problems with conditional amnesty.

First, they found that it was punitive. That is, it sought retribution against those who found war, and in particular the war in Viet Nam, immoral.

Secondly, it was unjust. That is, it allowed a deserter to return home, accept a military discharge and then be free to go. Whereas those classified as resisters or evaders would return to the United States, swearing an oath of allegiance as though they had never been citizens before, and then be faced with eighteen months to two years of alternative service.

Thirdly, and perhaps most interestingly of all because of its rather unselfish nature, is the fact that in no way did the program address itself to the unfairness of war and the fairness of resistance.

And yet, even with these problems aside for a moment, let us look at the astounding revelation that just seven weeks ago came from the United States Justice Department when it released for publication a list of 4400 names of some 148,000 young men still eligible for conditional amnesty. Now this significantly exacerbated the problem since as the Justice Department had pointed out only those persons whose names appeared on this list could be followed up and prosecuted under the law. This clearly demonstrated that prosecution at best would have been discriminatory and highly ineffective. And yet, with this information available to it, the present administration continued to sail a course with little rudder to guide it.

The question we might ask then in view of these problems: Is there a simple and equitable way that we might resolve them? Let us turn to the words of some Americans here at home, in order that we might get a more balanced perspective on this question.

The historian Henry Steele Commager expresses his view in terms of society when he writes, "If the war in Southeast Asia is a mistake from which even now we are extricating ourselves, is it just that we should punish those who at whatever cost helped dramatize that mistake. If we are to restore harmony to our society and unity to our nation, we must put aside all vindictiveness, all inclinations for punishment, all attempts to cast a balance of patriotism or of sacrifice as unworthy a great nation."

And the final statement is from Mr. Robert Ranson, father of one of the 50,000 young men who gave their lives in the rice paddies in Viet Nam. Mr. Ranson feels that those who lost their sons in Viet Nam can view the war with a perspective that is simply not available to the rest of us. And he writes: "As we come to grips with the grim reality of what has gone on in the minds and consciences of those who have left the country, deserted, or gone to jail, it would be most gratifying to me if I felt that I could have contributed in any small measure toward the granting of the broadest kind of general amnesty, one without penalties and conditions."

Then if I may paraphrase a former president of the United States as he said to us all for the purpose of national unity, "Let's put Watergate behind us." I would urge Americans today let's put Southeast Asia behind us. Certainly not in the humanitarian sense, but we have seen that America's military role in Southeast Asia is over. We remember the bombing halts, the negotiated settlement with Hanoi in January of 1973, the gradual withdrawal of American troops, the return of our POW's, the evacuation of thousands of South Vietnamese, and yet today tens of thousands of young Americans remain exiled on foreign soil all in the name of a lost crusade.

In keeping with these views we can see that the equitable and realistic solution is a universal unconditional amnesty for all Viet Nam–era resisters, evaders, and deserters. Now opponents to this position have said well, what of America's military morale. Or suppose that once again the United States were called upon to raise a large standing army. Would not the adoption of such a policy impede these? In response let me say that unconditional amnesty is nothing new to the United States. After World War I and World War II there was a granting of unconditional amnesty. Indeed after this country's Civil War there was a granting of an unconditional pardon and amnesty to all the confederate leaders who had been found guilty of treason in an effort to perpetrate an overthrow of the Union. So please realize with me then there is no need to concern ourselves with this faction of alarmists who would put forth such arguments. This is simply not the case. Notice also in our history that never when the national interest of the United States has been threatened have we failed to muster the troops.

Still others have said well, how can anyone support an unconditional amnesty and claim to be a loyal American. As a veteran of three years in the military, having served at a time when Viet Nam was at its height in terms of conflict, I too asked myself that question. Then I was unable to support such a position, but as I began to read and research this issue, coupled with what I saw happening to my country and my exiled countrymen, I came to the realization that my differences of belief with these men should not serve as their chains of bondage. Still other critics have asked well, what then are the logical arguments for the support of unconditional amnesty? Unfortunately, none. If vindictiveness is to be esteemed more than compassion; none, if the logic which drove young Americans from our country is the very same logic which will govern their return. And certainly none if humanitarianism is to be used only as an instrument of our foreign policy.

I had hoped by now to be able to abandon the necessity to discuss this issue of unconditional amnesty. No, not because it lacks significance or because of the ubiquitous nature of the amnesty question, but rather because by now I had hoped that America would have come to the realization of its futile battle against those who opposed an even larger futile war. Unfortunately for them, their war is not over. And I shall continue to speak for their freedom as I would for the freedom of all of us here today. As Americans join in making our political leaders aware that our humanitarian aid should continue to be extended to Viet Nam refugees, we should also make our political leaders aware that those in exile must also be treated in the humanitarian way. It is time to put an end to casting blame solely on those who resist the war, whatever their motives. Just as we open our homes and our homelands to those thousands of Viet Nam refugees, can we not find it in our hearts to open our homes and homelands to those thousands of young Americans still exiled from their country.

In considering these thoughts, we should all be reminded of Mrs. Peg Mullen, a gold star mother of Viet Nam who lost her only son in that war. Mrs. Mullen currently heads up the Amnesty Now program, calling for a universal, unconditional amnesty. And she asks us all the question, "What difference is there between a country which causes its dissidents to exile and a country which exiles its dissidents."

Appendix B: Gilkinson Personal Report on Confidence as a Speaker Scale*

Name _____ Instructor _____

Date _____ Sex _____ Age _____ The following material

has reference to _____

Check the following scale to indicate your feelings just before and at the beginning of a speech.

extremely frightened and confused	frightened, doubtful of ability	somewhat worried but willing to talk	a little nervous but eager to speak	entirely confident and eager to talk

1 _____/_____ 2 _____/_____ 3 _____/_____ 4 _____/_____ 5 _____

Check the following scale to indicate your feelings during the balance of the speech.

1 _____/_____ 2 _____/_____ 3 _____/_____ 4 _____/_____ 5 _____

Check all of the following terms which represent your feelings and experiences. Use column 1 to indicate feelings and experiences just before and at the beginning of speech. Use column 2 to represent feelings and experiences during the balance of the speech.

1	2	1	2
_____ trembling	_____	_____ nervous	_____
_____ sweating	_____	_____ dislike to look at audience	_____

*Howard Gilkinson, "Social Fears as Reported by Students in College Speech Classes," *Speech Monographs* 9 (1942): 144–47.

	1	2		1	2
	dry mouth	_____		fear of forgetting	_____
	rapid heart beat	_____		anxious to finish	_____
	blushing	_____		feel sickish	_____
	short breath	_____		emotionally upset	_____
	tense throat	_____		frightened	_____
	tense face	_____		anxious	_____
	tense body	_____		uneasy	_____
	lose ideas	_____		jittery	_____
	mental confusion	_____		embarrassed	_____

Circle "Yes," "No," or "?" for all the following statements:

1. Yes No ? Audiences seem bored when I speak.
2. Yes No ? I feel dazed while speaking.
3. Yes No ? I like to pick out some friendly person in the group to whom to address my remarks.
4. Yes No ? I am continually afraid of making some embarrassing or silly slip of the tongue.
5. Yes No ? My face feels frozen while speaking.
6. Yes No ? I have a deep sense of personal worthlessness while facing an audience.
7. Yes No ? Owing to fear I cannot think clearly on my feet.
8. Yes No ? The prospect of facing an audience arouses mild feelings of apprehension.
9. Yes No ? I get up to speak with the feeling that I shall surely fail.
10. Yes No ? While making a speech I feel more comfortable if I can stand behind a table.
11. Yes No ? While preparing a speech I am in a constant state of anxiety.
12. Yes No ? I feel exhausted after addressing a group.
13. Yes No ? My hands tremble when I try to handle objects on the platform.
14. Yes No ? I am almost overwhelmed by a desire to escape.
15. Yes No ? I am in constant fear of forgetting my speech.
16. Yes No ? I dislike to use my body and voice expressively.
17. Yes No ? I feel disgusted with myself after trying to address a group of people.
18. Yes No ? I feel tense and stiff while speaking.
19. Yes No ? I am so frightened that I scarcely know what I am saying.
20. Yes No ? I hurry while speaking to get through and out of sight.
21. Yes No ? I prefer to have notes on the platform in case I forget my speech.

22. Yes No ? My mind becomes blank before an audience and I am scarcely able to continue.
23. Yes No ? I particularly dread speaking before a group who oppose my point of view.
24. Yes No ? It is difficult for me calmly to search my mind for the right word to express my thoughts.
25. Yes No ? My voice sounds strange to me when I address a group.
26. Yes No ? I feel more comfortable if I can put my hands behind my back or in my pockets.
27. Yes No ? My thoughts become confused and jumbled when I speak before an audience.
28. Yes No ? I am completely demoralized when suddenly called upon to speak.
29. Yes No ? I find it extremely difficult to look at my audience while speaking.
30. Yes No ? I am terrified at the thought of speaking before a group of people.
31. Yes No ? I become so frightened at times that I lose the thread of my thinking.
32. Yes No ? My posture feels strained and unnatural.
33. Yes No ? My legs are wobbly.
34. Yes No ? Fear of forgetting causes me to jumble my speech at times.
35. Yes No ? I am fearful and tense all the while I am speaking before a group of people.
36. Yes No ? I feel awkward.
37. Yes No ? I perspire while speaking.
38. Yes No ? I gasp for breath as I begin to speak.
39. Yes No ? I perspire and tremble just before getting up to speak.
40. Yes No ? I am afraid the audience will discover my self-consciousness.
41. Yes No ? I am afraid that my thoughts will leave me.
42. Yes No ? I feel confused while speaking.
43. Yes No ? I never feel that I have anything worth saying to an audience.
44. Yes No ? The faces of my audience are blurred when I look at them.
45. Yes No ? I feel that I am not making a favorable impression when I speak.
46. Yes No ? I find it extremely difficult to stand still while speaking.
47. Yes No ? I feel depressed after addressing a group.
48. Yes No ? I always avoid speaking in public if possible.
49. Yes No ? I am in a state of nervous tension before getting up to speak.
50. Yes No ? I become flustered when something unexpected occurs.
51. Yes No ? I lose confidence if I find the audience is not interested in my speech.

52. Yes   No   ?   Although I talk fluently with friends I am at a loss for words on the platform.
53. Yes   No   ?   My voice sounds as though it belongs to someone else.
54. Yes   No   ?   At the conclusion of the speech I feel that I have failed.
55. Yes   No   ?   I look forward to an opportunity to speak in public.
56. Yes   No   ?   I like to experiment with voice and action to produce an effect upon an audience.
57. Yes   No   ?   I usually feel that I have something worth saying.
58. Yes   No   ?   I seek opportunities to speak in public.
59. Yes   No   ?   I am fairly fluent.
60. Yes   No   ?   I feel elated after addressing a group.
61. Yes   No   ?   I can relax and listen to the speakers who precede me on the program.
62. Yes   No   ?   I am not greatly disturbed if I think the audience does not agree with me.
63. Yes   No   ?   I find it easy to move about on the platform.
64. Yes   No   ?   My mind is clear when I face an audience.
65. Yes   No   ?   I have no fear of facing an audience.
66. Yes   No   ?   Public speaking is my favorite hobby.
67. Yes   No   ?   Unexpected occurrences while speaking do not fluster me.
68. Yes   No   ?   I have no serious difficulty in following the outline of my speech.
69. Yes   No   ?   I feel poised and alert when I face an audience.
70. Yes   No   ?   I enjoy preparing a talk.
71. Yes   No   ?   I feel relaxed and comfortable while speaking.
72. Yes   No   ?   I like to observe the reactions of my audience to my speech.
73. Yes   No   ?   I like to use humorous stories and anecdotes.
74. Yes   No   ?   I have a feeling of alertness in facing an audience.
75. Yes   No   ?   Ideas and words come to mind easily while speaking.
76. Yes   No   ?   Although I do not enjoy speaking in public I do not particularly dread it.
77. Yes   No   ?   I do not mind speaking before a group.
78. Yes   No   ?   I like to speak deliberately thinking my way through my subject.
79. Yes   No   ?   Although I am nervous just before getting up I soon forget my fears and enjoy the experience.
80. Yes   No   ?   I feel satisfied at the conclusion of the speech.
81. Yes   No   ?   It is interesting to search for effective ways of phrasing a thought.
82. Yes   No   ?   I have a feeling of mastery over myself and my audience.
83. Yes   No   ?   At the conclusion of a speech I feel that I have had a pleasant experience.
84. Yes   No   ?   New and pertinent ideas come to me as I stand before an audience.

85. Yes No ? I face the prospect of making a speech with complete confidence.
86. Yes No ? I take pride in my ability to speak in public.
87. Yes No ? Audiences inspire me.
88. Yes No ? Audiences seem interested in what I have to say.
89. Yes No ? Speaking in public is pleasantly stimulating.
90. Yes No ? I feel purposeful and calm as I rise to speak.
91. Yes No ? I feel expansive and fluent while before an audience.
92. Yes No ? I take greater pleasure in speaking than in any other activity.
93. Yes No ? I am not disturbed by the prospect of speaking in public.
94. Yes No ? Speaking in public is an exciting adventure.
95. Yes No ? I am neither excited nor frightened by the prospect of speaking in public.
96. Yes No ? I seldom have any difficulty finding words to express my thoughts.
97. Yes No ? I feel that I am in complete possession of myself while speaking.
98. Yes No ? I forget all about myself shortly after I begin speaking.
99. Yes No ? Although I do not enjoy speaking in public I usually accept an invitation to do so.
100. Yes No ? Speaking in public is a pleasurable experience unaccompanied by any doubts or fears.
101. Yes No ? I thoroughly enjoy addressing a group of people.
102. Yes No ? Audiences seem friendly when I address them.
103. Yes No ? At the conclusion of my remarks I feel that I would like to continue talking.
104. Yes No ? I find the prospect of speaking mildly pleasant.

Appendix C:
Evaluation Forms

SPEECH EVALUATION FORM

Name _____ Date _____

Assignment_____ Grade _____
(5-Superior, 4-Excellent, 3-Average, 2-Fair, 1-Poor)

Criteria	Rate 1–5	COMMENTS
CONTENT		
ORGANIZATION		
LANGUAGE USAGE (Style)		
AUDIENCE ADAPTATION		
SPEAKER ENTHUSIASM FOR TOPIC		
BODILY ACTIVITY		
USE OF VOICE		
GENERAL EFFECTIVENESS OF SPEECH		
TOTAL		

OTHER COMMENTS:
(Continue on back of page.)

This critique was completed by _____.

SPEECH EVALUATION FORM

Name _____ Date _____

Assignment_____ Grade _____
(5-Superior, 4-Excellent, 3-Average, 2-Fair, 1-Poor)

Criteria	Rate 1–5	COMMENTS
CONTENT		
ORGANIZATION		
LANGUAGE USAGE (Style)		
AUDIENCE ADAPTATION		
SPEAKER ENTHUSIASM FOR TOPIC		
BODILY ACTIVITY		
USE OF VOICE		
GENERAL EFFECTIVENESS OF SPEECH		
TOTAL		

OTHER COMMENTS:
(Continue on back of page.)

This critique was completed by _____.

SPEECH EVALUATION FORM

Name _____ Date _____

Assignment_____ Grade _____
(5-Superior, 4-Excellent, 3-Average, 2-Fair, 1-Poor)

Criteria	Rate 1-5	COMMENTS
CONTENT		
ORGANIZATION		
LANGUAGE USAGE (Style)		
AUDIENCE ADAPTATION		
SPEAKER ENTHUSIASM FOR TOPIC		
BODILY ACTIVITY		
USE OF VOICE		
GENERAL EFFECTIVENESS OF SPEECH		
TOTAL		

OTHER COMMENTS:
(Continue on back of page.)

This critique was completed by _____.

SPEECH EVALUATION FORM

Name _____ Date _____

Assignment_____ Grade _____
       (5-Superior, 4-Excellent, 3-Average, 2-Fair, 1-Poor)

Criteria	Rate 1–5	COMMENTS
CONTENT		
ORGANIZATION		
LANGUAGE USAGE (Style)		
AUDIENCE ADAPTATION		
SPEAKER ENTHUSIASM FOR TOPIC		
BODILY ACTIVITY		
USE OF VOICE		
GENERAL EFFECTIVENESS OF SPEECH		
TOTAL		

OTHER COMMENTS:
(Continue on back of page.)

This critique was completed by _____

EVALUATION FORM FOR INFORMATIVE SPEECH

I felt frustration because the information presented exceeded my comprehension capability.

	1	2	3	4	5	6	7	
Strongly agree	——	——	——	——	——	——	——	Strongly disagree

I experienced fatigue because the amount of information exceeded my attention span.

	1	2	3	4	5	6	7	
Strongly agree	——	——	——	——	——	——	——	Strongly disagree

I experienced low motivation because the information was uninteresting or because the information was presented without constant reinforcement of attention.

	1	2	3	4	5	6	7	
Strongly agree	——	——	——	——	——	——	——	Strongly disagree

I experienced resistance because the information was revealed in such a way that made me avoid, attack, or mentally compete with the information.

	1	2	3	4	5	6	7	
Strongly agree	——	——	——	——	——	——	——	Strongly disagree

OVERALL REACTION TO THE SPEECH

	1	2	3	4	5	6	7	
Poor	——	——	——	——	——	——	——	Superior

SPEAKER _____ Critiqued by _____

EVALUATION FORM FOR INFORMATIVE SPEECH

I felt frustration because the information presented exceeded my comprehension capability.

	1	2	3	4	5	6	7	
Strongly agree	___	___	___	___	___	___	___	Strongly disagree

I experienced fatigue because the amount of information exceeded my attention span.

	1	2	3	4	5	6	7	
Strongly agree	___	___	___	___	___	___	___	Strongly disagree

I experienced low motivation because the information was uninteresting or because the information was presented without constant reinforcement of attention.

	1	2	3	4	5	6	7	
Strongly agree	___	___	___	___	___	___	___	Strongly disagree

I experienced resistance because the information was revealed in such a way that made me avoid, attack, or mentally compete with the information.

	1	2	3	4	5	6	7	
Strongly agree	___	___	___	___	___	___	___	Strongly disagree

OVERALL REACTION TO THE SPEECH

	1	2	3	4	5	6	7	
Poor	___	___	___	___	___	___	___	Superior

SPEAKER _____ Critiqued by _____

EVALUATION FORM FOR INFORMATIVE SPEECH

I felt frustration because the information presented exceeded my comprehension capability.

1   2   3   4   5   6   7

Strongly agree ___ ___ ___ ___ ___ ___ ___ Strongly disagree

I experienced fatigue because the amount of information exceeded my attention span.

1   2   3   4   5   6   7

Strongly agree ___ ___ ___ ___ ___ ___ ___ Strongly disagree

I experienced low motivation because the information was uninteresting or because the information was presented without constant reinforcement of attention.

1   2   3   4   5   6   7

Strongly agree ___ ___ ___ ___ ___ ___ ___ Strongly disagree

I experienced resistance because the information was revealed in such a way that made me avoid, attack, or mentally compete with the information.

1   2   3   4   5   6   7

Strongly agree ___ ___ ___ ___ ___ ___ ___ Strongly disagree

OVERALL REACTION TO THE SPEECH

1   2   3   4   5   6   7

Poor ___ ___ ___ ___ ___ ___ ___ Superior

SPEAKER _____ Critiqued by _____

EVALUATION FORM FOR INFORMATIVE SPEECH

I'felt frustration because the information presented exceeded my comprehension capability.

	1	2	3	4	5	6	7	
Strongly agree	___	___	___	___	___	___	___	St ongly disagree

I experienced fatigue because the amount of information exceeded my attention span.

	1	2	3	4	5	6	7	
Strongly agree	___	___	___	___	___	___	___	Strongly disagree

I experienced low motivation because the information was uninteresting or because the information was presented without constant reinforcement of attention.

	1	2	3	4	5	6	7	
Strongly agree	___	___	___	___	___	___	___	Strongly disagree

I experienced resistance because the information was revealed in such a way that made me avoid, attack, or mentally compete with the information.

	1	2	3	4	5	6	7	
Strongly agree	___	___	___	___	___	___	___	Strongly disagree

OVERALL REACTION TO THE SPEECH

	1	2	3	4	5	6	7	
Poor	___	___	___	___	___	___	___	Superior

SPEAKER _____ Critiqued by _____

Appendix D:
Student Speech Analysis

Student Analysis

Student Speech

WIDOW, A HARSH AND HURTFUL WORD

Karen Eaton

Parkersburg Community College, West Virginia

Coached by Cathy Beaty

Janet Markusic and her husband Frank had managed the University Union 76 Service Station in Columbus, Ohio, since 1961. The lease with the Union Oil Company was, of course, in Frank's name. Then, in June of 1974, Frank died, and Janet took over management of the station full time. But Union Oil immediately terminated her lease.

Managing a service station was the only way 41-year-old Janet knew of supporting herself and her five children. but she was given two weeks to vacate the station.

Union Oil officials stated that they "weren't really trying to take food out of the mouths of a widow and her children," but were merely concerned that she might not be able to manage a full-time business while trying to care for her children, and they gave the lease to a man. I can't help but wonder what would have happened if Janet had died. Union Oil's assumption would still be valid—Frank would be caring for the children alone, but I doubt they would have cancelled his lease.

"Widow" is a harsh and hurtful word. It is derived from the

*Reproduced from *Winning Orations.* Mankato, Minnesota: The Interstate Oratorical Association, 1976.

Sanskrit and means "empty." And that's what our society believes a widow to be—if not empty, then not whole. Lynn Caine, author of the book Widow, believes that our society is set up so that most women lose their identities when their husbands die. These are the women who have spent their entire married lives in the home, having few identity-establishing experiences of their own. For these women, and they are in the majority, marriage is a symbiotic relationship—they draw upon and exist in the reflection of their husbands. But what happens when a woman's husband dies?

Perhaps to many of you even marriage is in the future, so why should you be concerned about the death of your spouse now? Perhaps you still have both your parents and the only widows you know are elderly eccentric women who have withdrawn from the world around them. I think it's time we face the reality of death and begin thinking about its effects on the living.

Widowhood becomes a reality for 2½ million women in the United States each year according to the Bureau of the Census. The 1970 Census further reports that 1 out of every 6 women in this country over the age of 21 is a widow—and only 1% of the widows remarry. The average age of a woman when widowed is 42. If you are a woman, the chances that your marriage partner will precede you in death are five times greater than if you are a man. No, widowhood is not something reserved for the elderly who are just waiting to die, too.

My own mother became a widow eight years ago at the age of 41. She was left with two children aged 14 and 19, and no work experience during her 21 year marriage. I have discovered that my mother's plight was typical of many younger, middle-aged widows. My father, like so many men of his generation, believed that his wife should never work as long as he was able.

Student Speech

What are the major problems confronting the new widow? I can sum it all up in one word—discrimination, both socially and economically. Socially, a widow becomes taboo. At a time when she needs friends most, they want her least. Dr. Richard Conroy, a psychiatrist at St. Luke's Hospital in New York City made a study of this phenomenon, and found that it was almost "customary" for married women to drop widows socially, even if they had been good friends. The widow is an unwanted reminder that this could easily happen in our lives. Also, Dr. Conroy believes the married woman begins to see her own widowed friend as a competitor, possibly after her own husband. Ironically, however, for the 2 million widowers in the United States today, the challenge seems to be staying single. According to the Retirement Guide, published by the American Association for Retired Person, most widowers, rather than being socially ostracized, are the object of matchmaking and endless proposals from women eager to do their cooking, yard work, and household chores.

The discrimination and ostracism against the widow socially give her time to dwell on her grief, which is something she certainly doesn't need, and time to dwell on her economic discrimination, another problem usually not faced by the widower.

A lot of time, expense, and confusion can be avoided if the husband would leave a will. But according to the Widow Study, prepared by a consortium of life insurance companies, more than 70 percent of the husbands die without doing so.

The widow must also check to see if her husband's company provides her with a survivor's pension. A 1968 Bureau of Labor

Student Analysis

Statistics study of one hundred select plans—mostly large ones with supposedly liberal provisions—found only forty-four with automatic death benefits. Even under plans that do provide a survivor's benefit, it usually goes to widows only under certain conditions and only if the husband has followed certain complicated procedures.

Also, the widow must sign up for Social Security benefits. This will probably result in a lump sum benefit, the maximum of which is $255. And that's all she gets, unless of course, she has dependent children under the age of 18, or 22 if they're still in school. But even that monthly benefit is usually not enough to live on, so the widow suddenly finds herself thrust into the job market, where she finds even more discrimination.

Dorothy Kosta, a special writer for the Denver Post, suggests to widows that they lie about their age, tint their hair—well, generally just cater to America's youth culture. It is a sad comment on our time that mature, reliable women have to resort to deception in order to make a living—and the living they make isn't much of one. Their average salary, according to the Census Bureau, amounts to $5,342 a year, just above the national poverty level. If the widow is receiving monthly Social Security benefits, however, the most she can make without losing those benefits is $2,520.

The social and economic discrimination, which comes at a time when the woman is least able to handle it, can be devastating. But what can be done about it?

To bring an end to social discrimination, we must first change our attitudes on death and widowhood. Perhaps our schools would be a good place to start. We now find classes in our schools on marriage and family living, so why not a class on death and bereavement? As it is now, we seldom accept the fact of our own mortality, and can't accept a

Student Speech

death when it occurs in the life of someone we know. This is especially true of attitudes toward widows, since they are the one single largest group whom death has touched. Just because a woman's husband dies is no reason to condemn her to a social death. But this is a long-range solution to discrimination. What of the 12 million widows in America today? For them, a care-line type service should be established. This would give the new widow, who finds herself shut-off from her friends, a sympathetic ear to turn to. One agency, called "Widowed Services," has been established at the University of Oregon. The agency has helped hundreds of widows with a variety of problems from being a friend to informing them of their rights and responsibilities, but now is running low on funds and may have to close soon.

In reference to the widow's economic discrimination, one of the most vital things which must be done is to liberalize private pension plans and government benefit systems. A man who has worked all his life paying into a pension plan through his job, and paying into Social Security should not leave a financially destitute widow.

As for jobs, some steps have been made to help the middle-aged woman who suddenly needs to work. It is now illegal to ask a person's age on a job application, but that doesn't help during an interview. According to Carol Powers in her pamphlet Your Widowhood Guide, employers need to realize that the most mature person, especially a widow, can be the best employee. She needs and depends on her job more, so she will probably be one of the company's most loyal employees. My mother was one of the relatively lucky ones. She was able to take adult education courses and re-educate herself on some of the

Student Analysis

skills she had before her 21 year "retirement." Many women don't have this chance.

Perhaps by the time my generation reach middle age, they won't have to face the social and economic discrimination so prevalent today. Maybe . . . but until then, remember the words of Lynn Caine. "I do not want to be pigeon holed as a widow. I am a woman whose husband has died, yes. But not a second-class citizen, not a lonely goose." Widow is a harsh and hurtful word. Only we, by acting now, can change its meaning and perhaps our own future.

Appendix E:
Visual Aid
Checklists

Name _____

VISUAL AID CHECKLIST

Type of Visual Aid (Check the type of Visual Aid you intend to use)

_____ Chart
_____ Graph
_____ Diagram
_____ Map
_____ Object
_____ Cartoon
_____ Print
_____ Photo, Slide, Filmstrip, or Film

Media Forms (Check the media form you intend to use)

_____ Poster board and felt-tip pen
_____ Transparency
_____ Photo, Slide, Filmstrip, or Film
_____ Opaque Projector (would be consistent form with pen, film, transparency)
_____ Audio

Review each question below and initial when you have completed each

_____ 1. Have you chosen material carefully?
_____ 2. Have you checked the size of the visual aid?
_____ 3. Is the visual aid clear and easily understandable?
_____ 4. Have you prepared material to "keep you talking" while you use the visual aid?
_____ 5. Have you taken precautions to be certain the aid does not become the speech?
_____ 6. Have you rehearsed with any equipment you plan to use?

Name _____

VISUAL AID CHECKLIST

Type of Visual Aid (Check the type of Visual Aid you intend to use)

_____ Chart
_____ Graph
_____ Diagram
_____ Map
_____ Object
_____ Cartoon
_____ Print
_____ Photo, Slide, Filmstrip, or Film

Media Forms (Check the media form you intend to use)

_____ Poster board and felt-tip pen
_____ Transparency
_____ Photo, Slide, Filmstrip, or Film
_____ Opaque Projector (would be consistent form with pen, film, transparency)
_____ Audio

Review each question below and initial when you have completed each

_____ 1. Have you chosen material carefully?
_____ 2. Have you checked the size of the visual aid?
_____ 3. Is the visual aid clear and easily understandable?
_____ 4. Have you prepared material to "keep you talking" while you use the visual aid?
_____ 5. Have you taken precautions to be certain the aid does not become the speech?
_____ 6. Have you rehearsed with any equipment you plan to use?

Name _____

VISUAL AID CHECKLIST

Type of Visual Aid (Check the type of Visual Aid you intend to use)

_____ Chart
_____ Graph
_____ Diagram
_____ Map
_____ Object
_____ Cartoon
_____ Print
_____ Photo, Slide, Filmstrip, or Film

Media Forms (Check the media form you intend to use)

_____ Poster board and felt-tip pen
_____ Transparency
_____ Photo, Slide, Filmstrip, or Film
_____ Opaque Projector (would be consistent form with pen, film, transparency)
_____ Audio

Review each question below and initial when you have completed each

_____ 1. Have you chosen material carefully?
_____ 2. Have you checked the size of the visual aid?
_____ 3. Is the visual aid clear and easily understandable?
_____ 4. Have you prepared material to "keep you talking" while you use the visual aid?
_____ 5. Have you taken precautions to be certain the aid does not become the speech?
_____ 6. Have you rehearsed with any equipment you plan to use?

Appendix F:
Persuasive Speech
Preparation Checklist

Name _____

PERSUASIVE SPEECH PREPARATION CHECKLIST

Check or fill in each blank as you complete each step.

1. _____ Topic selection (check here when you have answered the five questions below)
   - _____ Is the topic suited to the audience?
   - _____ Are you comfortable with the topic?
   - _____ Are you motivated by the topic?
   - _____ Is it an unusual (not "overworked") topic?
   - _____ Do you think you can find sufficient information on the topic?

   If you answered *no* to any of the questions above, you may experience problems with your topic. Reconsider your topic selection.

2. What is the point of persuasion; or what attitudes, opinions, or actions are you attempting to change?

   _____

   _____

   _____

3. _____ Audience Analysis: Have you considered the wants, needs, and values of the audience in relation to your speech?

4. _____ Major points selected

5. _____ Supporting material to be used (check below first)
   (Check here when this section is completed.)
   - _____ Non-artistic proofs
     - _____ Statistical information
     - _____ Quotations
     - _____ Specific examples
     - _____ Illustrations
   - _____ Artistic proofs
     - _____ Emotional
     - _____ Ethical

6. Is the supporting material:
   _____ relevant to the topic?
   _____ as direct as possible?
   _____ representative of various types of support?

If you answered *no* to any of the above, reconsider your supporting material.

7. Check for references you have used to locate supporting material:
   _____ Encyclopedia (General)
   _____ Card Catalog (for books)
   _____ Readers Guide to Periodical Literature (for magazines)
   _____ Education Index (for magazines)
   _____ Other—indicate source: _____

_____

If you have not checked three or more of the above, review this step.

8. _____ Have you recorded information on note cards or in another retrievable form?

Name _____

PERSUASIVE SPEECH PREPARATION CHECKLIST

Check or fill in each blank as you complete each step.

1. _____ Topic selection (check here when you have answered the five questions below)
   _____ Is the topic suited to the audience?
   _____ Are you comfortable with the topic?
   _____ Are you motivated by the topic?
   _____ Is it an unusual (not "overworked") topic?
   _____ Do you think you can find sufficient information on the topic?

   If you answered *no* to any of the questions above, you may experience problems with your topic. Reconsider your topic selection.

2. What is the point of persuasion; or what attitudes, opinions, or actions are you attempting to change?

   _____

   _____

   _____

3. _____ Audience Analysis: Have you considered the wants, needs, and values of the audience in relation to your speech?

4. _____ Major points selected

5. _____ Supporting material to be used (check below first) (Check here when this section is completed.)
   _____ Non-artistic proofs
       _____ Statistical information
       _____ Quotations
       _____ Specific examples
       _____ Illustrations
   _____ Artistic proofs
       _____ Emotional
       _____ Ethical

6. Is the supporting material:
   _____ relevant to the topic?
   _____ as direct as possible?
   _____ representative of various types of support?

   If you answered *no* to any of the above, reconsider your supporting material.

7. Check for references you have used to locate supporting material:
   _____ Encyclopedia (General)
   _____ Card Catalog (for books)
   _____ Readers Guide to Periodical Literature (for magazines)
   _____ Education Index (for magazines)
   _____ Other—indicate source: _____
   _____

   If you have not checked three or more of the above, review this step.

8. _____ Have you recorded information on note cards or in another retrievable form?

Name _____

PERSUASIVE SPEECH PREPARATION CHECKLIST

Check or fill in each blank as you complete each step.

1. _____ Topic selection (check here when you have answered the five questions below)
   _____ Is the topic suited to the audience?
   _____ Are you comfortable with the topic?
   _____ Are you motivated by the topic?
   _____ Is it an unusual (not "overworked") topic?
   _____ Do you think you can find sufficient information on the topic?

If you answered *no* to any of the questions above, you may experience problems with your topic. Reconsider your topic selection.

2. What is the point of persuasion; or what attitudes, opinions, or actions are you attempting to change?

   _____

   _____

   _____

3. _____ Audience Analysis: Have you considered the wants, needs, and values of the audience in relation to your speech?

4. _____ Major points selected

5. _____ Supporting material to be used (check below first)
   (Check here when this section is completed.)
   _____ Non-artistic proofs
      _____ Statistical information
      _____ Quotations
      _____ Specific examples
      _____ Illustrations
   _____ Artistic proofs
      _____ Emotional
      _____ Ethical

6. Is the supporting material:
   _____ relevant to the topic?
   _____ as direct as possible?
   _____ representative of various types of support?

   If you answered *no* to any of the above, reconsider your supporting material.

7. Check for references you have used to locate supporting material:
   _____ Encyclopedia (General)
   _____ Card Catalog (for books)
   _____ Readers Guide to Periodical Literature (for magazines)
   _____ Education Index (for magazines)
   _____ Other—indicate source: _____
   _____

   If you have not checked three or more of the above, review this step.

8. _____ Have you recorded information on note cards or in another retrievable form?

Name _____

PERSUASIVE SPEECH
MAJOR POINT DEVELOPMENT FORM

Speech Topic: _____

I. Major Point: _____

   A. Sub-Point: _____

Type of
supporting
material:

Supporting material: _____

   B. Sub-Point: _____

Type of
supporting
material:

Supporting material: _____

   C. Sub-Point: _____

Type of
supporting
material:

Supporting material: _____

Name _____

PERSUASIVE SPEECH
MAJOR POINT DEVELOPMENT FORM

Speech Topic: _____

I. Major Point: _____

A. Sub-Point: _____

Type of supporting material: Supporting material: _____
_____
_____

B. Sub-Point: _____

Type of supporting material: Supporting material: _____
_____
_____

C. Sub-Point: _____

Type of supporting material: Supporting material: _____
_____
_____

Name _____

PERSUASIVE SPEECH
MAJOR POINT DEVELOPMENT FORM

Speech Topic: _____

I. Major Point: _____

_____

A. Sub-Point: _____

_____

Type of   Supporting material: _____
supporting   _____
material: _____

B. Sub-Point: _____

_____

Type of   Supporting material: _____
supporting   _____
material: _____

C. Sub-Point: _____

_____

Type of   Supporting material: _____
supporting   _____
material: _____

Index